# RECOLLECTIONS

OF

# CHILDHOOD;

OR,

## SALLY, THE FAITHFUL NURSE.

BY

### PRIMOGENITA,

ONE OF THE CONTRIBUTORS TO THE "PENNY SUNDAY READER."

*"From grave to gay, from lively to severe."*

LONDON:
HATCHARD AND SON, PICCADILLY; SEELEY, FLEET STREET;
RIVINGTONS, ST. PAUL'S CHURCH YARD.
CANTERBURY:
WARD, MERCERY LANE.
BRISTOL:
LIGHT AND RIDLER, AND CHILCOTT.

1840.

TO THE

## DEAR LITTLE GIRL,

WHOSE HOURS OF SUFFERING WERE SOMETIMES BEGUILED

BY THE RELATION OF THE SIMPLE EVENTS DETAILED IN THE

### Following Pages,

## THEY ARE DEDICATED,

WITH A THANKFUL HEART, AND WITH EARNEST PRAYERS FOR

HER PRESENT AND EVERLASTING WELFARE,

BY

## THE AUTHOR.

# INTRODUCTION.

A very simple introduction may possibly suffice for a very simple volume. I have aimed at nothing more than an innocently entertaining book for children. Will it be objected that there are many such already? I know there are,—hundreds, perhaps thousands—but mine is a new one. It occurred to me some time since, to have the care of a dear little girl, during a tedious illness; and a new book was a great prize to us. There were times too, when none of our many books would do, and then I leaned over her, and in a low voice told her many of the simple events recorded here. Should my book prove entertaining to any dear sick child, its end will be answered. If I could have written what children call "a Sunday Book," I should have felt myself on higher ground, and perhaps should have been more useful, but I have done that which I felt most equal to. Is any further apology required? I was *invited* to write,—rather an uncommon thing in these days. Other reasons I have none. My tale as to its main incidents is a true one; its very simplicity proves it, and I am in reality what my signature bespeaks me,

PRIMOGENITA.

*May,* 1840.

# RECOLLECTIONS OF CHILDHOOD;

## OR

## SALLY, THE FAITHFUL NURSE.

We hear much of the ingratitude of servants,—their independent spirit, and the little hope of their becoming attached to the families with whom they dwell; and there may perhaps be much ground for such assertions: the spirit of the age no doubt has its influence in the kitchen, and the servants hall; and the cheapness of articles of luxury and taste, makes our female servants (in towns at least) very fine ladies. Our parlour maids, and this is fact, have their rose-wood work boxes, and their albums; and our cooks draw on their lace gloves, encircle their necks with a boa, and step forth, in general appearance at least, little inferior to their mistresses. Alas! Alas! the day of black worsted stockings and checked aprons is nearly gone;—yet notwithstanding, I do believe there remain many attached and faithful servants,—*servants* still—doing their duty humbly and heartily, in that state of life in which it has pleased God to place them. And besides this, I do believe many a family has its SALLY,—the friend of forty years, who having lived long in their regular and quiet household, having taken one little one after another from a month old, having tended those children in sickness, and played with them in health, has so fixed on them *her* affections, and so established herself in *theirs*, that a tie has been formed between them not to be loosened as long as they continue here. One such instance at least I know, and *our* Sally's history, though a simple one, has the charm of truth.

"You will get all ready for your master, he will come home on Friday evening." So ended a letter to Sally, when she was the only inmate of a small parsonage in a very retired village. I could shew you my kind reader a sketch of that village; its grey tower, the dashing waters of its rustic mill, its precipitous bank crowned with a row of pretty cottages, and its willowy pond. We have pointed to one and another among the more imposing of those humble dwellings, and have asked, "Was that the house?"—No Miss, no,—Sally has said—"Master has'nt drawn it, but it must be there, near the church, among the trees." There it was, and there perchance it still is, but I cannot describe it, because though it was my childish boast that I was the only one who had been at H——, my triumph was often repressed by the rejoinder, "Ah! but you were only six months old, so you cannot remember it! No, I cannot remember it, nor can I tell you exactly how its inmates looked, but fancy loves to be busy here. Sally's master came, young, lively, intelligent, with a sparkling eye, and a deep toned silvery voice, and a kind and courteous word for all, and a heart warm in *his* master's cause. But I cannot trust myself here, and besides, it is Sally's story

I am telling. She was young *then*, slight and active, neat, I am sure she was, in her person, and in all with which she had to do,—and for her costume, if you are young, my reader, I can remember in that, some things you never heard of. Her brown hair was long, even in front, but combed smooth, and then ingeniously turned back in a sort of large flat loop upon her forehead, the whole surmounted by the neat crimped border of her thick muslin cap; her gown of dark print was open in front, and curiously looped back, disclosing a glossy stuff petticoat, and the sleeves of this gown extending only to the elbow, were so tight, that I well remember as a child, watching with interest the daily operation of binding a broad ribbon round the arm, to be again dexterously withdrawn when the gown sleeve had been pulled over it. With this style of gown an apron was indispensable,—mostly of check, but on very special occasions, of stout Irish;—tight round her throat Sally then wore a narrow black ribbon, and years afterwards when the fashion, for such I suppose it was, no longer prevailed, there remained where the ribbon had been, a streak of white, telling that that throat had been fairer once. Years after this she asked her kind *mistress's leave* to buy a white dimity petticoat, and two pair of cotton stockings. Altogether, Sally was the very pattern of a trim and useful servant.

Well, Sally got all ready for her master. She was of a humble and rather anxious turn of mind, and it was not without some trepidation that she fulfilled her three-fold office of housekeeper, cook, and waiting maid. In after times she used often to amuse us by recounting some of her mistakes.

It was not long however that the sole responsibility rested upon Sally. Her mistress came,—but I tread lightly here. The grave has closed upon that beloved one: "her children rise up and call her blessed, her husband also, and he praiseth her," and in their hearts is her best memorial; wherefore, though for many long years she ruled with wise and gentle government, and Sally served with duteous fidelity, there will be but slight and incidental mention of her in these pages.

And now the humble subject of my *true* story, set herself with alacrity to fulfil her regular and daily tasks. That first twelvemonth was the least varied perhaps of her life, but probably not the least happy. To rise day by day with work to do, and health and strength for its fulfilment, to pass quietly on in the path appointed for us, in the performance of common place, and every day duties, is a state of life not perhaps much envied, but full at least of the ingredients of happiness, and so improved by many, as to produce its fruits in as much perfection as we can expect to cull them here below.

But that first year has glided imperceptibly away, and with the birth of the welcome baby, the first of the train of children that Sally loved so well, her duties and employments were changed. It was pleasanter to trust the little helpless being to one of tried care and fidelity, than to a stranger; and Sally's affectionate temper led her to be well pleased with the arrangement.—The baby!—Oh what pleasant thoughts, what a long perspective of loving cares does the word conjure up! From the very first hour, the admiration of the important nurse, and the delight of the mother, how does its influence widen and extend; well loves the father, long before he ventures to handle the tender little thing so mysteriously wrapped in fold after fold of calico and flannel, well loves he to gaze on it, in its little spotless cot, or better still in its mother's tender arms, and to call it his own. Then come the servants in on tip toe, to wish their mistress joy, and to pronounce it the finest child they ever saw,—then, if it be mild pleasant weather, in some few days the little thing is carried round the garden, or to and fro before the house ; and the careful nurse gently throws back the mantle, that the old gardener, or some favoured neighbour may have a peep;—until at length, on the happy day of the christening, it comes forth in all its glory, in the very best robe, the satin hood, and the triple rows of costly lace, half hiding the little soft red face they are intended to adorn; and, only of less consequence than the nurse, is admired by clerk and sexton, the squire's lady, and the village children. Then back in its quiet nursery, its gay trappings laid aside, how loves the tender mother to press it to her bosom, and kiss its soft soft cheek, and lift her eye and heart in prayer and thanksgiving to *Hannah's* God. Pardon me, kind reader, this long digression.—I am very fond of babies, the very sight of the little flannel cap, wakens in my mind a thousand pleasant thoughts, but I spare you and proceed.

It was not very pleasant perhaps to the inmates of the quiet parsonage, to leave the village of H——— for a residence in a distant city, to give up a country house with all its pleasant occupations, its garden, and its fields; and to establish themselves in one, which though larger indeed and more commodious, had little to boast of as to situation, and whose

narrow slip of ground behind, scarcely deserved the name of
a garden. And yet I am wrong,—that home of my childhood
was pleasant too; although in a street, there were no houses
opposite, but instead, a large and pleasant bowling green,
where many a man of wealth and consequence repaired on
summer afternoons, to enjoy a sport, *now* I believe nearly
exploded. Then on the other side of the house, the windows
commanded a pleasant and extensive view of hill and dale,
and there being no streets beyond ours, the access into the
country was short and easy; so that upon the whole, though
some years after, this residence was again gladly exchanged
for one in the country, there was much in it pleasant and
agreeable: and well it was that the voice which in the little
church of H——— had sounded the glad tidings of salvation
to the few rustic worshippers assembled there, should now
pour forth its flood of persuasive eloquence, in a larger
temple and to a far more numerous audience.

Now then commenced Sally's city life,—she was farther
from her native home, and could expect to see her father
and mother but at intervals, and for a short time, but
this was not reason enough for quitting her comfortable place;
so with the baby in her arms, and its young mother by her
side, she commenced the somewhat long journey. There
were those expecting them at its close, who had no *common*
interest in the travellers; who would look with especial interest on the baby. And Sally was aware I think, how lasting are
first impressions, and in order that the little first-born might
make one in every respect favourable, the chaise was stopped;
and seated on a bank, under a spreading tree, on that spring
morning the kind nurse arrayed the infant in a clean cap and

robe, arranged its little cloak and bonnet, and expected it to create no small sensation.

Now from this time the history of those she served seems so interwoven with hers, and so many incidents recur to the mind in reviewing the days of childhood and youth, that I fear I may be thought somewhat discursive. Pardon me, kind reader, in these digressions. Many are the simple pleasures of children brought up at home, many the pleasant memories that hang around the scenes familiar then; around nursery, field, and hill side; and profitable perhaps the reflections upon such scenes, which the experience of later years suggests. Pardon me therefore, and as a child goes forth in the pleasant spring-tide, with some definite object,—to gather perhaps daisies or primroses,—but is lured on from flower to flower, and returning home, shakes from its little basket in bright abundance flowers of every hue, periwinkles, hawthorn, cuckoo flowers, and butter cups in gay confusion ;—so suffer me to cull and treasure up as they recur, the happy incidents and memories of youth.

But little change occurred in the circumstances of my dear nurse for several years; her cares and responsibility increased as one after another was added to her little charge. Our kind parents gave up the drawing room for a nursery, and this airy and pleasant apartment was the scene of many a game of hearty play. We were very happy; Sally's authority was generally sufficient to keep us in good order, but in case of any very heinous offence, a reference was made to our parents, for as dear Sally once said,—"I never gave one of you a slap in my life my dears."—Then the kind father, who mostly looked so cheerful, put on a dark grave look, and commanded the little culprit to follow him to his study,—no trifle this, for the study was a small room at the very top of the house,—he walked very slowly up, and an awful thing it was, as we followed, to reflect on what might occur when we got there; but I believe nothing ever did occur, beyond a long grave lecture on the one hand, and a copious flood of tears and earnest promises of amendment on the other.

How succeeded this mild and gentle training? Did reverence mingle with the love the children of such a father bore him? In after years was a *word*, yea or *look* of his, sufficient for their guidance? Did a ready prompt obedience grow out of his gentle bearing towards them? I hope—I think, I may say that it was so.—Does the eye of a *parent* glance over my page? Oh be ever gentle with the children God has given you; watch them constantly; reprove them earnestly, but not in anger : in the forcible language of Scripture, "Be not *bitter* against them." "Yes, they are good boys," I once heard a kind father say, "I *talk* to them pretty much, but I do not like to *beat* my children : the world will beat them." It was a beautiful thought, though not elegantly expressed. Yes, there is not one child in the circle round your table,— healthful and happy as they look now,—on whose head, if long spared, the storm will not beat. Adversity may wither them, sickness fade, a cold world frown on them, false friends forsake them ; but amid all, let memory carry them back to a home where the law of kindness reigned, where the mother's reproving eye was moistened with a tear, and the father frowned more in sorrow than in anger.

I said we had an easy access to the country, and many were the pleasant walks we took with Sally. There was one in particular, through some pleasant fields shadowed by lofty elms; how many a little bunch of daisies did we gather there. It led by a mill-stream over a high gate, and through a broad gravelled road, till we came to the Asylum for Orphan Girls, with its simple but pretty chapel, and its row of tall poplars. I have been there since, and but for the chapel, which yet remains, and which, with its row of regular windows and fairy spire, was so impressed on my memory,—but for these, I could scarcely have believed I was treading the same ground. The quiet retirement of those pleasant fields was gone;—a large and imposing building had been erected for the orphan children in place of the irregular but quiet and comfortable house they occupied before,—and row after row of freestone houses, extending between it and the city, had for ever banished all country sights and sounds. The children and nursemaids in our old street, for children and nursemaids I doubt not there are there still, must go farther now for a country walk.

There was another way;—up the steep ascent crossed with streets to the very summit, and relieved here and there by flights of steps; up this steep way we climbed with weary feet, turning round now and then, to see the growing city beneath us—then when we had reached the very top, fresh was the breeze, and pleasant the extended view of hill and dale, the broad woods, and blue mountains beyond. Nearer, immediately beneath us, lay the extended city, with its wilderness of roofs, a dark but imposing mass, relieved here and there by patches of dingy green, marking its squares, with

their rows of ancient trees,—by its glass houses, to our childish fancy, grand as the Pyramids of Egypt,—and by its sixteen or eighteen noble churches. And yet I doubt if all this
pleased us so well as the walk along the topmost street ; for
here in front of a row of irregular houses, were some strips of
garden, gardens the most beautiful we ever saw then;—long
narrow patches bright with flowers, (for the air was purer and
freer from smoke than in the city below) adorned some of
them, with trees fantastically cut, and some with urns and
sun-dials, and small images on pedestals: and yet perhaps
these gardens would not have pleased us so well had they
been fully exposed to view : walled they were, and enclosed
with doors, but in most of these doors was a square or an
oval opening, filled up with a sort of iron fillagree work, and
there was a charm and mystery in peeping through these
apertures at the varied gardens, and the pretty houses to
which they belonged, and never did our kind Sally refuse to
wait for us, and to lift us up again and again for another
peep ; till with the last we came to the termination of the
long street, and ran out delighted upon the smooth turf of a
high hill, one broad green field leading away through an
avenue of stately trees, and a stone archway, to a princely
mansion, the termination of our pleasant walk. In that field
is now erected one of our light and spacious modern churches,
to which, from its situation, and the serpentine church path
marked out on that wide hill-side, its long train of worshippers
may be seen afar off, advancing in troops, "A multitude
that keep holiday, walking to the House of God as friends."

But I think I must relate a few particulars of the very
pleasantest walk of all, and this was to the Farm. It was

not so often with Sally though, that we went there, neither did we *all* go—I do not know that the whole party would have been at all times acceptable visitors, but if the truth must be told, I believe that *I*, Sally's *first* charge, was as the eldest, an especial favourite there. It was with my dear father mostly, that I took this long walk through the very midst of the city to its other extremity. Sometimes too I was a guest for days, and even weeks together at the Farm; and I fear on my return, poor Sally sometimes found, that neither my temper, nor my manners, were improved by the too great indulgence I received there. And yet there is much very pleasant connected with my memory of the Farm, and the kind friends who loved me so well. And who lived at the Farm? I fancy my young reader enquiring. Why only an old gentleman and lady, Molly and Patty, and the gardener, and a long train of cows and geese and fowls, &c., a very important part of the menage. No *child* did I ever see there, nor do I think I took many of my playthings, and leaving dear parents and merry playmates, and Sally behind, I almost marvel that I accounted it so great a treat to go there.

Perhaps you will take a greater interest in my old friends if I describe them. They had in some measure supplied the place of parents to our dear father, and "Grandpapa" and "Grandmama," were the names of fond familiarity we had learnt to bestow on them. Grandpapa, then, was a tall and portly man, assiduous in business, and of some standing among the merchants of the city; full of kindly feeling to all, and as the event proved, only of too easy a temper. I remember him in his pew at church, dressed, as indeed he always was, with the nicest care, standing erect, and responding with loud voice all through the Psalms; his eyes fixed on a very large prayer book, placed upright on the seat opposite him. I remember at that time settling it in my mind, that he was not only a very kind, but a very good man,—a point on which I believe children who have been rightly trained will generally be found very anxious. Alas! if later and more discerning years produced painful doubts on this point, if there were darker shades in the character of that kind old man, it would little become me to dwell on them. We cling to every hope for those we have loved well. There were three silent days preceding his death, during which he lay quite in the possession of his faculties, but saying little or nothing. I think it is Cowper who beautifully observes, "Much may pass within the curtains, between the dying sinner and his God, which the doctor and the nurse little dream of". To his God we must leave him, but Oh how blessed to lay our beloved ones to rest in sure and certain hope of their joyful resurrection to life eternal; to know that weary and heavy laden with their sins, they sought rest, and found it even here; to know, that they built upon a rock, and that rock was Christ.

> " Lift not thou the wailing voice,
>   " Weep not, 'tis a christian dyeth ;
> " Up where blessed saints rejoice,
>   " Ransom'd now the spirit flyeth.
>
> "High in heaven's own light she dwelleth,—
> " Full the song of triumph swelleth;
> " Freed from earth and earthly failing;
> " Lift not thou the voice of wailing."

These doubts and reflections, however, of later years little disturbed me then. Certainly I most dearly loved that kind old couple. I wonder I was not completely spoiled by them, for though my Grandmamma (for I must call her so) often repressed the injudicious indulgence of her husband towards me, yet I think in her way, she was little better.

But I have not described her. In person she was large and tall, with strongly marked and expressive features: her hair was *more* than grey. In a little brooch I wear, it looks like the softest white silk. It was very long, and often have I seen her favourite servant comb it smoothly down, till it looked like spun glass,— so even and fair and glossy; then she would turn it up in a long fold, and fasten it with a small comb of dark tortoise-shell ;—but alas! for the sentiment of the thing, there was tied over the whole a front of false hair curled and powdered, and again surmounted by a cap of very primitive shape. I do not know that there was any thing else very remarkable in her dress, for she conformed pretty much to prevailing fashions, but every thing was very ample. I remember having to hem round the skirt of a black silk gown,—breadth after breadth,—I thought it would never be done. In her latter years, when I best remember her, she was crippled and confined to the house, and mostly indeed to the sofa, and though nice and appropriate, her dress was simple : but there was a certain high chest of drawers, (Oh how often I wished I could rummage it thoroughly) and many were the stores contained there;—stiff silks and rich tabinets, broad gay ribbons, and multitudes of the little soft Italian flowers, once I believe much in vogue, and very costly. She ministered, I fear, to my childish vanity, by arraying me in some grotesque finery, unknown at home. In particular, I remember a frock she made me, out of a broad striped muslin, wherewith I wore a wide old-fashioned red and brown ribbon, as a sash, bright yellow shoes, and a gay necklace, which the kind old gentleman had bought for me, (fire-stone, I think he called it),—and thus arrayed, he pronounced that I looked " something like."—Later still, I remember on one occasion, when they took me home in their carriage, after a visit to them, that I sat as forward as possible, on the very edge of the seat, in order that as we drove down the long village street (for we lived in the country then) my neighbours and acquaintances might have a full view of my new bonnet, with gay pink ribbons. Altogether I think it must have been with trembling that my dear parents parted with me on these occasions. Certainly it was only my return to their judicious and steady management, that counteracted the ill effects of my very different training at the Farm.

But will you go with me round the Farm? Perhaps I fancy I remember much which is only familiar to me through the valued sketches made there at the time by a dear and skilful hand. I turn over leaf after leaf in that pleasant memorandum book, and much that would otherwise have escaped me is recalled vividly to my mind. The house was very unpretending; an old building, improved by the addition of two good rooms, commanding an extensive prospect. These rooms I then thought very spacious, and greatly admired the wide sofa with its gay chintz covering; the mirror with its circle of bright balls, and golden eagle; the brass fender so scrupu-

lously nice, and the soft white rug ; but all I fancy was on
a very simple and moderate scale, and the furniture was somewhat scanty, and chiefly such as might be spared from the
town house, where our old friends lived the greater part of
the year. One thing I distinctly recollect admiring then,
and should admire now, a row of noble balsams, so placed in
a window as for the light to stream through their long smooth
transparent stems, and on the purple and pink and white of
their waxlike and beautiful flowers. So strong is the power
of association, that I do not think I have ever seen a balsam
from that day to this, without being reminded of those, neither
have any since appeared to me quite so beautiful. The garden
was abundant in flowers,—nothing rare,—anemonies, lupines,
sweet peas, old fashioned sweet smelling flowers, and roses of
many varied kinds ; but I loved to wander farther than the
garden into the pleasant quiet fields around. One occasion
in particular I remember, when I wandered round with old
Hannah as my guard : I suppose no one else was at liberty.
Now old Hannah was a short fat old market woman, with a regular cotton bedgown, and a broad flat hat, suited to the
heavy burdens she had to carry. I remember often thinking
the old woman rather dirty, but she was very good tempered :
neither do I think (and children are pretty quick observers)
that there was any thing coarse in her manner or expressions.
Well, away we went and found some cowslips, and plenty of
daisies and golden cups, but of primroses, my especial admiration, we could see none, till in one field, fenced off alas !
by a hedge and deep ditch, on a green and sunny bank, grew
the beautiful flowers in rich abundance, shining like stars
amid their dark green leaves. There was a little country girl

in the field all alone gathering them, and the old woman
asked if I might come in. "No," she said, it was a long way
round to the stile, and besides, her father was very particular,
and never let any body go into his field, but she would pick
me some;—here was a fresh dificulty, we could not reach them,
and if thrown over untied, away they would go into the ditch,
but my old companion with woman's ready invention bethought her of a remedy. She whipt off her garter, (I see it
now, the broad grey selvage of a coarse flannel,) rolled and
looped it into a sort of ball, and jerked it over the hedge;
the kind little girl shook out her lapful of primroses on the
grass, sat down, arranged, and tied them up, and over they
came, a noble bunch, which I bore home in triumph, and I
dare say valued the more for having procured them with
some difficulty. You will think I am a long time at the farm,
and yet I cannot leave it without introducing you to Patty.
Patty was the cook; a dark, stout, plain featured welsh
woman : but Patty was a great friend of mine; never the
rival of my dear Sally, no, that could not be, I should have
felt indignant at such an insinuation, but yet I was very fond
of Patty: she let me follow her every where,—dairy, kitchen,
fowls' court, pig sty, away we went daily through them all :
then when she made a plum pudding, she let me sit on a high
stool, and stone the raisins, and she gave me barley for the
fowls, and water for my garden, and defended me from my
only enemy, the gander. Besides all this, she admitted me
even to her bed room. She had a large chest filled I dare say
(for she had been long in respectable service) with sundry
substantial gowns, and aprons, and petticoats : these I cared
little about, but on one side near the top of the chest was

fastened a long narrow sort of box, with a cover to lift up, filled with Patty's treasures;—shells, and bright jumbee beads, pieces of pretty money, and heart pincushions, rolls of ribbon, double nuts, and curious little boxes. It was a gay variety, and I fear I coveted my neighbour's goods; certainly though I have been admitted since to the cabinets of the curious, the boudoirs of the rich and tasteful; certainly I have never admired the treasures there, as I did that strange medley in Patty's little deal box. One thing more quite won my heart: on a sunday morning, or on any particular occasion, when she was to appear in her best, she let me *dress* her as I called it. Her best gown was a tabinet, a sort of tea colour, the gift probably of her mistress. Now gowns at that time of day *were gowns*; they fastened in *front*, and this one was cut round and low, and drawn with a running string, and it was a great treat to me, standing on a chair, to draw it even, and tie it over Patty's double handkerchief of stiff clear muslin: then the band was to be pinned, and so long was the operation all together, that Patty would declare, she really should be too late at church, and I must please to let her finish. Poor Patty! Our intercourse after all had a very sudden termination. She went out one morning before breakfast, and on her return the quick eyes of her fellow servants discovered a bit of rag tied round "the fourth finger of the woman's left hand." Patty said she had a sore finger, perhaps she might, it was all mystery to me then, but I have since suspected that she had on her finger under the rag, that which has sometimes produced, if not a sore finger, a broken heart: at any rate, from that day she vanished from the scene. She lived long in my memory and affections, but I saw her no more, nor even ever heard what became of her.

Dear old farm! I think the only thing that troubled me
very much, was my Grandpapa's shooting at the sparrows;
not through pity for them I fear, but mere dread at the report
of his gun. We would walk round and round on a quiet
summer evening, he gun in hand, but under a faithful promise not to let it off, till a flock of the mischievous birds
feasting on his fruit or vegetables excited him beyond en-
durance,—he must shoot, he really must. "Well, let me run
in first," and away I would fly, scampering over bed and
border, and rushing into the quiet drawing room, where
Grandmama usually sat, and falling on my knees before her,
would muffle up head and ears and all in the ample folds of
her gown ; she calling me a silly little puss, but declaring in
the same breath, that it was a pity to terrify the poor child.
Dear old farm ! Never shall I forget the confused sensation
of delight which I used to experience at waking on the first
morning after my arrival there, when all the unaccustomed
country sounds,—the lowing of the cows in the near barton,
the blithe crowing of the cock, and the whetting of the scythe,
mingled with my morning dreams, till I opened my eyes to
the glorious daylight, and to the happy certainty that I was
really at the farm.

But where did I leave Sally? Shall I be forgiven for
losing sight of her so long? During these my several visits,
she was pursuing her quiet and orderly path, most occupied
of course, with the one who at that time was the *baby*, but
making the nursery pleasant to all, by her care, and skill,
and untiring patience. She was always busy. Such work as
it rested with her to do, was regularly and promptly done;
and one there was dearer still, whose head was planning,

whose kind hands labouring for us. Our neat white bonnets of glazed muslin, all alike, our gingham frocks, with tippets and sleeves of the same; or in winter, our dark stuff frocks and beaver bonnets:—These are trifles when told, but on the orderly arrangement of such trifles depends the neat appearance of a little family, and the habits of order and economy which the several members of such a family may form.

How beautiful is order! and how discernible its effects. I would walk with you through a crowded street, and we would decide, not as a rather saucy young man did, how many *pretty* women, but what is of far more consequence, how many *tidy* women we met. I would take the rich and the poor, the old and the young; all may be either tidy or untidy. If bonnet strings, gloves and stockings will bear investigation, all the rest is pretty sure to be right. Tidy,—is a dear little English word: the girl so designated, is almost sure to make a neat, orderly, useful woman. "Go and put your drawers *tidy* my dear" says the careful Mother, and away trots the little thing, (not more perhaps than six or seven years old,) and first she opens one drawer after another, and stands somewhat abashed at the confusion they are in; and she thinks it was really only last week that she put them to rights; and she wishes drawers would *keep* tidy, but somehow or other, first she put in one toy for which she wanted a very safe place, and then another, and then her doll's straw bonnet, and then she threw in her own handkerchief and gloves in a hurry, till altogether, there certainly seems a great deal to be done before she can run back to her Mother and assert that her drawers are quite *tidy*. "Never mind little one, you will manage it by and by. Put your things all out on the bed, or on the chairs, and then begin."

It is a pretty sight. I love to see a little steady child helped on and encouraged in neat and orderly ways; but I think we should not be particular in making them do things just in *our* way. They have little plans and notions of their own, and if they are allowed to follow them out, they will take more interest in the business in hand. Time and experience will teach them a better arrangement if *we* can but induce the habit and love of neatness and order. I remember once being in a shop with a friend, and while she made her *purchases*, I made my *remarks* silently, and I hope not uncharitably, upon the various customers,—and one I cannot forget. A great fat untidy girl, her hair in papers, and gown half unbuttoned behind, *rushed* into the shop, thrust herself heedlessly between the ladies at the counter, asked for a skein of black silk, and tossing down a penny, darted away again, just saying "I suppose that will do." The neat young woman who had served her, smiled as she took up the penny, and I smiled too. There was something ludicrous about the transaction. It was not poverty made the girl look so wretched; her clothes though so miserably dirty, were substantially good, and her fat arms and cheeks told no tale of want. In imagination I followed her home; her expression implied that she was employed by another, and I could not but fancy her the untidy maid of a slatternly mistress, and, for the skein of silk purchased in such haste, it was probably I thought, to sew a button on the coat, or draw up a hole in the stocking of the unfortunate master of the house. Alas! How many poor girls leave the house of an untidy *Mother*, for that of an heedless *mistress*, and grow up in habits of sloth and carelessness never to be unlearned.

But I have made a long digression on one of my favourite virtues: with thankfulness I confess that *we* were brought up in an *orderly* manner. There was order in assembling at prayers in the morning, and in our daily walk with Sally, order when we sat round the table with our dear parents in the pleasant winter evenings, with our work, and pencils, and picture books, beautiful order when one by one, morning and evening, we went alone with our dear Father to the neat and quiet room where he taught us the words of thanksgiving and prayer.

Sally loved to see us *nice*, though we were never *fine*, and looked perhaps with a little pride on her young ladies, when, on any particular occasion, she set us off to the best advantage. Our dear parents, I rather think for our sakes, entered but little into society, but I can remember once or twice, the curtains being drawn, and the candles lighted in the best parlour, in preparation for company; then, on a little low form, sat I and two dear sisters, anxiously waiting the arrival of the guests, and fully resolved to be very good children. Dear Sally! it was a simple amusing testimony that one of us bore to her care. The little thing on some occasion, went out alone to dinner: a great event, especially as her entertainers were persons of some style and consequence. After dinner, finger glasses were placed, a thing to which we were unaccustomed, and in fact had never seen. The child's wondering eyes followed one and another lady as they immersed their finger tips in water, and wiped them with the doily. At length some one kindly said, "Will you dip your fingers in before we go up stairs?"—"No thank you Ma'am," said the little girl, "Sally washed my hands before I came." The lady smiled, as well she might, but the child wondered why, and little thought she had said any thing *outré*.

But time passed on, and Sally's value was to be proved in the day of trial.—The shutter closed, in her hitherto happy nursery, was to tell of a faded flower. We had a little brother, full of spring and life, though only five months old, but he sickened and died, and bitter were the tears the parents shed over their only son; then after a time another was born, and of him too the Saviour said "Suffer him to come." A brief week or two was all his span of life, and for three days he lay, as Sally expressed it, panting like a little bird, so still and motionless, that she stooped down from time to time, to feel if he yet breathed. Blessed angels! ye who thus outstripped us in the race, ye first in heaven! I love to dwell upon the thought, that it was mercy took ye there so soon; and that the same mercy, free and unmerited, will guide and guard those that remain, and carry them, if it be even to hoar hairs.

> " Now with footstep soft and slow,
> " From thy narrow grave we go;
> " Rest, thy pleasant journey's ended.
> " Ere the morning sun ascended,
> " Ere the toil of busy day,
> " Thee thy master called away:
> " Giving thee just time to tell,
> " Christ loves little children well."

I think it was only this last baby whose little wax-like corpse I saw. The darkened room, the little coffin covered with grey cloth, the closed eyes, the soft flannel dress tied at the wrists with white satin ribbon, those little marble hands— Oh how present it all is even now to my memory ! It was the first time I had seen a corpse, but I have seen many since,— some among the poor ; I do not like to shrink from the sight, and it is often a pleasure to the poor mother, and even to the widow, that you should see the orderly and neat arrangements they have struggled hard to make ;—turn not away,— it is humbling, painful, but it will help to lift your heart from earth to heaven.

And yet I once gazed on a corpse which I had rather not have seen, so vivid and painful has the impression been. A young person, a distant relation, who lived with the deceased lady, had accepted my offer of calling to see her, an offer which, though not intimate, circumstances rendered it fitting that I should make, and as I rose to leave her, she said, " Will you walk into the other room ?" I thought she might feel hurt if I declined to do so, and we went in. There, in a rich coffin, lay the poor decaying body, decked as in life,—the false hair, the blond cap, the costly gown, the satin shoes,—Oh it was a revolting sight. " Did she wish it?" I said. " O yes," said her young relation, with a mournful but calm look, " I hope I have done all she could have wished."

Is it too painful to dwell on ? Come then and see an aged christian in her last deep sleep. I loved to look on her, and to think that her long pilgrimage was ended : " All the days of my appointed time will I wait till my change come." Such

year after year, had been the feeling of that time worn christian ; and she *did* wait, until month after month of her unva-
ried existence gliding by, she numbered nearly a hundred
years. "I cannot hear you," she would say to the old friends
admitted in the morning to that large and well furnished
drawing room. "I cannot hear you, but I love to look at
you." No, she could not hear *us,* but there was one she could
hear, though with an effort painful to the speaker. Her admirable and excellent daughter—that lady-like, and sensible
woman, ever greeting you with her pleasant smile, ever ready
in some act of courteous kindness. "Tell me *any* thing" she
would say "for it all amuses my dear mother ;" not now," she
would quietly add, if we wished the dear old lady to partici-
pate in what passed. It was when her visitor was gone, that
that devoted daughter sat on a low stool at her mother's feet,
and with discriminating love, and untiring patience, repeated
of all that had passed, what would most interest her aged
auditor. It was a beautiful sight—but there were times when
there passed in that apartment a scene of still deeper interest,
when that aged lady who had been long unable to take her
accustomed place at the table of the Lord in His sanctuary,
required of her minister, as she very frequently did, that he
would come and spread it for her there. When, with her
daughter and an old domestic, they knelt in all humility, and
receiving the broken bread in remembrance of the body of
Christ, which was given for them, they fed on him in their
hearts by faith, with thanksgiving; when they drank the wine,
and remembered that Christ's blood was shed for them, and
were thankful. I have heard her minister say, that she was
always somewhat agitated on these occasions. Oh I marvel

not! Deemed she not that she might probably drink no
more of that fruit of the vine till she drank it new in her
Father's kingdom? Dwelt not her thoughts on angels and
archangels, and on all the company of heaven? And as she
rendered to God hearty thanks for all his servants departed
this life in his faith, and fear, who shall say what memories
arose in her mind who had trod the earth for nearly a century?
Who shall say how parents on whom the grave had long closed,
how children lost in infancy, how friends of later life gone
down before her to the quiet grave, passed then in review before her mental eye? Dear old lady!—yes, when the grave
clothes in all their neat simplicity shrouded those aged limbs,
when the plain border of snowy whiteness, shaded that calm
pale face, it was indeed solemn, but beautiful to look on her.

But where have those two little angel brothers led me?
I think it was after the bereaved parents had laid them in the
grave that their fears were again excited, and Sally's powers
as a nurse again called into exercise by the severe illness of
one of their elder ones. Long and carefully tended was that
cherished child. Earnestly offered up, and graciously answered were the prayers for her recovery; and a most kind and
patient nurse did dear Sally prove. How many ways did she
devise to amuse and interest! Hers was *heart service*. She
loved the children committed to her care, and that one I verily
believe she loved the better for those days of weariness, and
nights of watching. At length they passed, and Sally rejoiced,
scarcely less than the parents, in the recovery of the sick child,
" Sally has been very kind to you—you shall buy her a new
gown" and a guinea was put for the purpose into the little
one's hand. With the guinea a cotton print was bought, good

and substantial, there were no three and sixpenny dresses *then.* It was of a light colour because it was to be kept for best. I remember the pattern perfectly ; but that of another given to Sally twenty years afterwards, when she came to her sick child's wedding, I quite forget. She had the first gown then, perhaps she has it now. Fashions must have varied less in those days, for though Sally's summer gowns were unaltered from year to year, and with the bright Spring days came out as good as new, I do not recollect that she ever looked old-fashioned. *We* saw no fault in her, her dear familiar face had looked kindly on us as long as we could remember, and as to Sally's *going away*, it was a contingency we never so much as thought of, but alas ! the time was not distant, though we knew it not.

I do not think she was ever very strong, and about this time her health began to fail, and change of air was recommended. She was to go home for a time, and well I remember her coming early in the morning into the room where my dear parents slept, to take leave of them. She tried to make me laugh by asking me if she did not look " A funny figure," and she certainly did, for her kind master had given her his flannel dressing gown to wear on the journey. A cloak, I suppose, was to cover its grotesque appearance, but as it was, the long back and tight sleeves had certainly an odd effect, but I did not laugh. Sally went; and it was my first great trouble. For *many* a week we asked how Sally was, and when she would come back. "Oh she was better, she was almost well, but she could not come back yet." In vain we asked when she *could* come, in vain wondered why Sally staid so long at her mother's. At length the dreadful truth burst upon us, "Sally was married"! Did you know she was going to be married? "Oh yes, a long time ago." There was an end, then, of all our hopes; our kind parents reasoned with us, strove to comfort us, but it was a trouble that took more time to cure than children's troubles usually do. Our sorrow however was almost swallowed up in indignation when we found that Sally was married to a *blacksmith*: if it had been to a *carpenter*, we declared we should not have minded it near so much, a carpenter or any decent man, but a blacksmith! a man with a dirty leather apron, and his shirt sleeves tucked up to his elbows,—it was dreadful! When poor Sally came to see us some time after, I am sure we must have hurt her feelings very much, by the reflections we scrupled not to make upon her choice. It was in vain she told us that the forge was "right away like, under the walnut trees,"—in vain she hinted that it was a good business, and that George was very steady, and had made some little money already; in vain she described his nice Sunday suit, and told us he was reckoned quite respectable, and sat in the gallery with the singers,—no, it would not do; the facts of the case remained the same: our dear neat Sally was married to a *blacksmith*, and there was a want of poetical justice about the thing, to which we could by no means reconcile our minds.

I suppose that as being the eldest, Sally's loss made still more impression on *me*, than on the others,—certainly it was a sore and lasting affliction. I can remember standing on a dull day, looking out mournfully into the street, and my eyes filled with the tears that *would* come when I thought of Sally; my dear mother was there, Oh well do I remember

her gentle reproof; she said if I so grieved for Sally, *some*
might think (*she* never should) but *some* might think, that I
loved her even better than I did my father and mother; and she
added, that I ought to set my sisters an example of content
and cheerfulness. It was a word in season : I felt that there
were none on earth I loved as I did my dear parents, and
almost triumphed in the childish thought, that they *could* not
go away, and from that time my grief at any rate was more
moderate.

But what was to be done ? Happily Sally could write,
for her kind master had taught her in her spare hours during
that first quiet year at the village of H———, and I might
write to her as soon as I was able. Here was a spur to my
exertions. I devoted all my energies to get beyond round o's
and pot-hooks, and with the first attempt at join-hand was
begun the first epistle I ever wrote,—the commencement of a
correspondence which has been carried on for more than
thirty years. Large, and plain, and round, no doubt were
the characters in that letter, beginning probably with " My
dear Sally, I am very sorry you are gone,"—and after a few
brief sentences, ending as simply, but it sprung from a deep
and true affection ; the nurse of my childhood has been the
humble friend of my later years; there lives but one now,
who has loved me as *long* as Sally has, and though far apart,
yet if I survive her, I shall feel that I have lost one whose
place can never be supplied. " The friends of our youth are
going out one by one like evening lights, and we see none
rising to succeed them; none certainly ever can rise who
will be as good to us."

Well, Sally answered my letter. She was never much of a scribe, but still, a letter was a matter of less labour to *her* then, than to her young correspondent. *Now* Sally's hand is stiff and cramped, and her eyes are dim, and mine is comparatively the pen of a ready writer. Oh glorious time and place where such fluctuations shall be unknown!—where whatsoever faculty beseems that glorious existence, shall be perfect in its developement, and enduring in its power!

Pleasant was the country in which our dear Sally was located,—one which might be apostrophized in the beautiful language of the Poet,

" Land of brown heath and shaggy wood,
" Land of the mountain and the flood,—
" LAND *of my* SIRES"———

So might Sally add; she would scarcely perhaps enter into the sentiment so expressed, but the same feeling woke in her mind when she said, " It was very natural to go back to the old place," and one yet holier when she added, " It will be pleasant to be near mother, and help her a bit in her old age." " To be near Mother,"—how much does it imply: *near*, to ask the counsel none else can give, to pay the dear attentions none other can claim; *near*, to rejoice and to weep together, and in perplexity to take sweet counsel.

Now it was many years after Sally's marriage, that I saw her pleasant cottage, and the forge under the walnut trees; and it must not be supposed that all the comforts in which it abounded then, were to be found in it at *first*, but sure I am

that Sally would not have thought it right to begin house-
keeping, without having things comfortable about her. The
solid oaken table, and substantial chairs, the deal dresser, set
out with plates and jugs, the tea-waiter and pretty tea things
in the corner cupboard, and a store of saucepans and a bright
tea-kettle; all this I know there was. Sally's life has proved
her trust in the providence of God, and her submission to
His will; but it was *not* proved by blindly rushing into diffi-
culties, and calling it by the holy name of faith.

In a book recommended to me as suitable for the poor,
(and in some respects a very good book it was,) there caught
my eye an account of a young married couple, who after
meeting their friends on their wedding day, (these friends
having brought refreshments with them,) having read the
Bible and knelt in prayer, found when their friends had left
them, that the sum of threepence was all they had to begin
life with together. The anecdote was told as true, and the
pious faith of the parties commended; but surely so rash and
improvident a course, little deserved to be so designated.
Let some little provision at least be made. The healthy
young girl, equal at first to her share of exertion, may sink
down into the worn and feeble Mother. Let her *save* the
guinea *now* in her comfortable place, that she will not be
able to *earn then*: the money spent on a gay ribbon, or
gauze handkercheif, has often been wanted afterwards for a
loaf of bread.

Well, but all this is not very interesting to *young* readers,
and I should like to think that mine would be a favourite
book with children. Well then my dears, we got on pretty

well without Sally. I do not even recollect who succeeded her in our nursery, so that probably it was some one who made no great impression, either favourable or otherwise: indeed from this time we elder children were chiefly with our parents, and month after month passed away, till we were told that Sally had a baby.

Oh how glad we were! how glad I was, for it was a little girl, and named after *me*. How I wished I could see it, and how I planned in my own mind, as soon as ever it could walk, to make it a little coloured frock and a bonnet, (for I was always a great bonnet maker,) a pinbefore too, and a tippet; in fancy the little thing was fully arrayed, while in the mean time, a little shroud on earth, and a garment of dazzling light in Heaven, was all that baby needed. Very sorry we were when we heard that it was dead, and poor Sally (one of those tender hearted ones, whose ready tears spring so soon to the eye,) she was sorry too, when heavy-hearted but uncomplaining, she laid that little one in its quiet grave.

I think it must have been soon after this that she came to visit us. Often, we know not why, some particular day or event in our existence stands out from the rest, clear and defined, with its accompanying circumstances, and this was one of such; better remembered than some days, and those, days of interest too, which we have passed perhaps twenty years afterwards. Certainly it *was* an event that Sally should come. It so happened there was company to dinner, a circumstance of rare occurrence. On such occasions, we children appeared after dinner; but it seemed a time that

would never come, and very tedious was the interval spent in
the nursery: *now* however we begged *not* to go down.  Poor
Sally!  After her long journey how we climbed about her,
and kissed her, and then she knelt down before the fire, and
on a fork warmed some pancakes she had brought for us;
and then helped to dress our dolls as she used to do, and
made a beautiful pair of pointed green morocco shoes, bound
with pink ribbon.  Altogether, it was I believe one of the
happiest days of our lives.  I do not know how long Sally
stayed, for the memory may well be called treacherous; few
and isolated are the events it retains, and those alas! too often
of less importance than many of those which escape us.  Her
visit probably was short, for Sally was too useful a wife
not to be missed at home, but her heart yearned I do believe,
especially perhaps after the loss of her little one, to see again
the children she loved so well.  Such visits were repeated
from time to time, but they are the only occasions I imagine,
during her long married life, when she has been absent from
home.

It was about this time I think, that our residence in the
city terminated, and to our great delight we went to live in
the country;  and though we cannot take Sally with us, yet
I must introduce you to the pleasant village of Y——.
Beautiful was the ride thither, of twelve or fourteen miles,
through a rich and cultivated country.  Each village you
pass, and there are many of them, has its accompanying tower
or spire, its scattered cottages, with their pretty gardens, and
here and there its ancient cross of grey stone, stained with
lichen, and tufted with the light sprays of the elegant stone
fern.  Then from one village to another reached the quiet

hedge rows, the dark elm, or broad walnut-tree here and there shadowing the road, and green lanes or rustic stiles leading away to long long walks across the meadows. There were no railways any where then, and I do hope there are none *there* now. Oh! it is cruel so to mar the face of the beautiful country,—so to hurry on the traveller through scenes of surpassing interest, that he must not even try to look at them, lest his very senses should reel.

Well, pretty as the villages were through which the road lay, there was not one of them prettier than the one which was to terminate our ride, and form our happy residence. It is somewhat altered now; two or three staring houses have sprung up, and two or three shadowy trees have been cut down: but *then* from the substantial house with its sloping garden at the entrance of the village, to the thatched cottage below the church, there was scarcely one thing you could wish altered. As the eye glanced down the long perspective, one neat dwelling appeared after another, gay with its bright garden, or mountain ash; while towards the middle of the village, a broad acacia threw its branches all across the road, and showered down on it its silver blossoms. Then our own house,—the pretty parsonage, with its lime trees in front, and rows of sweet peas trained along under the parlour windows, and its large garden behind, its ponds, and its orchard and field. Oh it certainly was a very pleasant spot. Then *we* had *our* gardens along by the nut-tree walk—we were curious gardeners; I believe children usually are; ever altering the arrangement of our ground, toiling and transplanting, and thinking that our gardens would be very beautiful some time or other. "My flowers will *not* grow, James," said *one* of

c

us to the gardener: "No miss," James would answer, "and they never will grow while you do torment 'em so."

An odd man was James; a shining red face he had, and evermore a broad grin, for he was a good tempered fellow, and when he grinned, what teeth he displayed! he actually had two rows above and below, a complete double set, and regular they were, and white, especially in the apple season, for we children used to say, James was always eating apples; they were very abundant, he had only to stoop and pick them up, and I suppose he liked them, for the man's jaws were a regular cider mill: and certainly the effect on his wonderful teeth, surpassed that of the finest violet dentifrice. Poor James! his phraseology used to amuse us; the broad garden thistle was "varnegated despert," and the spreading scarlet poppies with their rich deep eye, he always would call "noble popes."

I do not think he ever looked grave, but at church. There, dressed in his sunday suit, his countenance composed to a becoming gravity, and his hair duly smoothed down, James looked quite another man, one of the many orderly and quiet worshippers in that noble country church. A pleasant congregation it was that assembled there; there was no "squire's pew," for we were not in the immediate neighbourhood of any great man: but the old oak seats were filled with substantial farmers, some being in the immediate neighbourhood, others coming from a distance, with their families, in the snug market cart, or on horseback with their trim wives behind them on a pillion. Then there were the labourers in their clean smock frocks, smoothing down their hair, and reverently bending down their heads as they entered the house of God. And the school children, boys and girls, kept in due order by the terrors of a certain white wand, (exploded now I believe) and carefully taught their duty to God, and their neighbour; as much perhaps as they needed to know.

It was a remarkably fine old church, and, differing in many respects from the one we had been accustomed to in the city, it much attracted our childish notice. Even the stray branch of ivy, which had crept in near the gothic window, and the bird that now and then would skim along through the lofty aisle, were objects of interest, and drew away our thoughts, I fear, from holier things.

It was seldom we saw any but familiar faces in that country church; but one day, a little after service had commenced, the door of our pew, which was a large one, was opened, and in came, I think it was three ladies, if not four, very stout, and, as we children thought, very grand indeed in appearance; and we saw by a glance from our governess, that we were to be particularly orderly, and quiet; so we disposed of ourselves in the smallest possible space, so as not even to touch the ladies' silk gowns; and found out the places again in our prayer books, and sat wondering who in the world they *could* be. Oh heedless childhood! how long suffering is the holy God, who bears so long with the trifling thoughts,—the vain imaginations,—the " foolishness" that "is bound up in the heart of a child." Well, the ladies walked with us down the green churchyard lane, and the preacher, whom they had come some distance to hear, with courteous

affability introduced them to the parsonage; and after a little
while, the handsome carriage drove up, the ladies spoke kindly
to us all as we clustered round the gate; entered their
carriage, and drove away: and then we were told they were
the Mistress Mores. Which was Mistress Hannah More, we
eagerly enquired, for of *her* we had heard most, and for her
as well we might, we felt especial reverence. Oh she was not
there! she seldom left home, but we had seen Mrs. Betty,
and Mrs. Sally, and Mrs. Patty More. And a wonderful
thing we thought it, and something worth telling, that they
had come some miles to hear our dear father preach, and had
sat in our pew. Mrs Hannah More I saw some time after,
and of course such an event impressed itself on my mind, and
the recollection gratifies me still. It was very condescending
in her to request my dear father (whom she was ever pleased
to receive) to bring his little girl with him; and well pleased
did I mount the pillion behind him, to travel to Barley Wood.
A ride in this primitive style was always a great treat to us.
The pillion to be sure, was somewhat large, being suited to a
grown person, but the rest for the feet was drawn up short, to
suit our height: the kind horseman strapped a leathern belt
around his waist, by which we were to hold:—the whole family assembled in the yard on the occasion, and happy was the
child whose turn it was to leave her lessons and her theme
behind, and skipping to the top of the *upping* stock, take her
dignified seat behind her dear father,—aye, and to this day I
can remember, not words of cheerful kindness only, but
words of wisdom,—"The wisdom which is from above, pure
and peaceable," which at such times the loving father would
teach his child.—Now if these rides were pleasant on ordi-

nary occasions, of course it was a most delightful thing to go
thus to see Mrs. Hannah More.—I recollect feeling a sort of
triumph, which I dared not embody in words, in the thought
that even my governess had never been there. I do not think
the ride was longer than three or four miles, but it seemed
quite a journey then; the more so for being in a direction
which was new to me; and when we reached the elegant
house and tasteful garden, great was my admiration of all I
saw, and deep the reverence with which I waited the entrance
of Mrs. H. More. At length the parlour-door opened, and
she entered,—a little lively old lady, with a quick speaking
eye; her head muffled up in a shawl:—this she quickly
threw off, and entered at once into lively conversation with
my companion. I was sent with her maid round the pleasure
grounds,—up and down beautiful slopes, away to a rustic
temple, clustered round with clematis and brier, and back
again to gaze with wondering admiration on the rare and
beautiful flowers blossoming in the more immediate neighbourhood of the house; till at length, a signal from my father,
who stood at one of the windows opening out on the lawn,
brought me back to the elegant apartment, and the presence
of Mrs. More. Then it was that that condescending lady
took the especial notice of me, of which I was long after accustomed to boast. She must, she said, present me with one
of her works. One of her sisters said "You can give her the
'Search after Happiness'."—How very exalted I felt, as she
replied, "Oh no,—that is a little thing; a mere child's book."
Of course then, *I* was not a mere child; and as I was just at
the age when children are most anxious to establish this point,
I was much delighted to have such an authority on the sub-

ject. She sent up-stairs for two volumes, her " Hints for the
Education of a Princess," wrote my name in them in her firm
sensible hand-writing; and then, after partaking of some
refreshment, back we went to relate all the circumstances of
that eventful morning. I fear I have been rather diffuse in
relating them here, but, my kind reader, this being my only
*blue stocking* recollection, I trust you will pardon me.

Alas! that gifted and christian lady closed not her eyes,
as probably she then expected to do, in that sweet retirement;
she lived to say meekly, "I have been driven from my paradise,
but not by angels." One beloved sister after another dropped
from her side, they went " hence and were no more seen," and
then (it is a sad and humbling but true tale) she became in
her defenceless old age, the prey of faithless and designing
servants. No humble friend, no faithful *Sally* was amongst
them, to maintain the authority of the mistress, and support
her in her rights; but there were those who heard the tale
with indignation, and gathered round her, and bore her from
the scene of that sad misrule, to a safer though less secluded,
and less beautiful home.

This great treat, " riding double" as it was generally
called, we enjoyed sometimes on a Sunday afternoon, when
our dear father was accustomed to officiate at a very small
retired village church. He did not go *every* Sunday, and
there were many of us to take our turns, so that the treat
came but seldom to each, and was the more valued. A quiet
ride was that through the long bowery lanes, and across the
common. Some four miles perhaps, we went without meeting
half a dozen persons, till at length we reached the hamlet,

composed of a farm house or two, a shop, a blacksmith's forge, and a few pretty cottages clustered round the little low whitewashed church. Inn, or even alehouse, I rather think there was none, at any rate I know that "Pleasant" our old mare, was always put up in a shed attached to the cottage of a nice old man and woman, who regularly came out to the hatch, to welcome and receive us. My father used to tell the old man he looked like a fine old apple : and so he did ; his cheeks so firm and so rosy red. He stood erect, and his voice was strong, but his snowy hair told of three-score years and ten. The old woman was a pattern ; her high starched cap, the crimped border kept close to the face, by the satin ribbon bound round the head ; her ancient stuff gown, and white apron ; the shawl, not quite meeting in front, but with precision pinned a little apart ; altogether formed a "tout ensemble," which the artist would view with delight. Kind old woman! how pleased she was, to lift us down from our elevated seat, take us into her neat kitchen, dust the chair that needed no dusting, and bring "little miss" a draught of milk, or cut her a piece of brown bread and butter. By the way, I should have liked her all the better, *then,* if she had not called me "little miss." The nice old couple duly took their places in church, where I believe the congregation was larger than the immediate neigbourhood would have afforded.

One seat I know was filled by a farmer's family from some distance, and I well recollect hearing it observed, how respectable farmer D———'s family always looked : indeed they did,—where *now* shall we find such a set of young women as assembled there? Farmer D——— had been twice mar-ried, but at this time he was a widower, and his eldest daughter kept his house. I think he had two sons, but I never heard much about them;—but daughters! I verily believe he had a dozen; and down they went in regular succession, from the staid eldest Miss D——, who kept the house, to Harriet, the slight young girl of fifteen, with her light unsunned complexion, and her wavy hair. Her grave elder sister said, "Harriet must take to caps soon." Perhaps it was more fitting, but it seemed almost a pity that she should grow so soon out of the girl. How well they looked at church! how unpretending, yet neat in their appearance! I hardly know whether they looked best in winter, with their drab great coats, and dark bonnets; or in summer, in the neat gingham gown, and cottage straw bonnet, with its pretty light ribbon. I do not mean to imply that all Farmer D——'s daughters might be seen in his pew at church. Oh no, one after another young neighbouring farmer, bethought him how useful a wife, a neat and duteous daughter was likely to make; and one after another of the olive branches round the father's table was transmuted in her husband's house, into the fruitful vine; —and then would follow the cares of married life, and often in her new home was the assistance of some kind unmarried sister asked for and obtained; so that it was only perhaps five or six of the old man's daughters, that were usually about him at the time of which I speak; and busy daughters were these. We went to see them I recollect, and how visible was their handy-work in the arrangement and order of that large establishment. Little do you know in town, dear children, of the delights of such a tea-drinking as we had at Farmer D——'s. Your neat frocks are put on, white or silk, and perhaps (I have known such things) your silk stockings, and satin shoes, and your hair is plaited behind or before, or *both*, and tied with long ribbons; and away you go in a fly, or a chair, to drink tea with some young companion. There will be one or two more little girls, and you will sit round and play birds and beasts, or loto, or my lady's toilet, and if you are all yielding, and good tempered, it will be very pleasant, and I am sure I do not wish to make you feel dissatisfied with such visits; but I only wish you could go every one of you, as we did when we were children, to drink tea at a farm-house now and then,

A glance was bestowed on our coloured frocks, and if much soiled, (for we were always kept nice) they were exchanged for the clean set belonging to the next week.—If on the contrary, it was pronounced that they " would do," we had only to put on our clean stockings, and stout leather shoes, newly blacked; comb our short smooth hair, wash our hands, and we were ready.—Then, away we went, a merry laughing set, at about three o'clock in the afternoon, and if it was any distance, we went in the cart behind old " Pleasant." Bump, bump over the deep ruts in the narrow lanes, catching at the hazel boughs and wild roses that sometimes swept our bonnets, and where the lane was most narrow, wishing in our own minds that we might meet a waggon, because we could not think what in the world James would do *then*. And then when we arrived, how cordial and pleasant a reception was ever bestowed on the clergyman's little family and their governess; how gladly we tumbled out of the cart, and told James to be sure and *not* come till seven o'clock, and then went flocking in through the large kitchen, to the room beyond, neither so large, nor so light, nor so comfortable, but

dignified with the name of the *parlour*. However, neither in
parlour nor in kitchen did we stay long,—there was so much
to be seen and done; we might go and feed the pigeons, and
the poultry; and see the pretty brood of yellow ducklings in
the pond, and the poor anxious mother-hen run cackling
round. And they were just going to " sar the calves," as the
laughing red dairy-maid called it; and we looked on with
wonder at the pretty calves standing on a high wooden stage,
and receiving the warm milk which this same dairy-maid dexterously slushed from a pail into their open mouths. I wondered *then*, and I wonder to this day, why calves should take
their meals in such an unnatural mode; but I suppose it is
the grazier's business.—Then we went into the yard, to see
the cows milked, being duly cautioned however, not to stand
too near, for "Cowslip" was vicious, and "Daisy" had a
nasty temper; however they all gave beautiful milk, and so
we thought, as the dairy-maid frothed it up high into the pint
cup our kind hostess had provided us with. Then we went to
the cheese room,—a long room literally floored with cheeses,
which we heard with wonder were every one of them turned
over every day; we might run to the end, over these cheeses
and back again. What queer things children like to do!
The dairy, and the bee-hives, and the barn, we saw them all,
and then back to the house to tea, and a very substantial
meal we contrived to make; the plates of brown bread and
butter disappearing in no time. Another run or two round
the garden and orchard; another meal (alas! for the whol-
somes) of great red apples, new plum cakes, and raspberry
or currant wine; and then, to our dismay, James and the
cart appeared in the distance, and we were very soon packed
nto it, and on our way home. Such a visit, among others,

was the one we paid to Farmer D ——— and his daughters.
—He was a large heavy man, a cripple ; I think he scarcely
moved at all from his great chair by the kitchen fire. I
called his daughters duteous, and they were so, and one
service they had to perform for their old father, which must
have required both skill and courage.—He loved to sit by his
kitchen fire, and they loved to see him there, in his old accustomed place, but to get him up and down stairs, had become
painful to *him*, and almost impossible to *them*; so in the
ceiling of the kitchen, a trap-door was made into his room
above, and duly every morning was he lowered down, and at
night hoisted up again, chair and all, by the united strength
of his fair daughters. It was done I suppose by means of
pullies.—I am not very mechanical, but I think it must have
been a very difficult, and rather nervous business. We
children would have " given the world" to see the operation,
but Miss D——— said, it was not her father's bed-time, so
we could only look wondering up at the trap-door, and fancy
how the old gentleman would look when they got him half-
way up.

There was one amongst these daughters of whom we knew
much more than of any of the others ; and when I think of a
*useful* person, I think of Mary D———. Where *trouble*
was, there *she* was found, and she would come *uncalled* ; " I
thought I might be wanted," she would quietly say, " and so
I came :" and ever welcome was her kind sympathy in joy or
in sorrow.

" We do too little heed each others pain,
" We do relax too much the social chain
" That binds us to each other ;—small the care
" There is for grief, in which we have no share."

So wrote one of elegant mind and deep affections; the circumstances of whose death, in a foreign land, we shrink from enquiring into too narrowly, lest we should be constrained to believe the very worst. So wrote she, and it is a sentiment we should lay to heart. What comfort can I give to day? What wound can I help to heal? are questions we should ask ourselves with each morning's returning light. "I never ask for her now, they always say she is much the same." Such was the heartless observation I once heard respecting a poor invalid. Oh poor human nature! Well may we pray, "Take away my heart of stone." Yes, I thought, "Much the same." Pressing her couch from day to day with weary limbs, and an aching head; bearing her weight of woe, passing with slow footstep from one room to another, and looking meekly out upon the pleasant fields she may never tread again. And do you never ask? Oh it is little enough we can do for the poor invalid;—a kind enquiry, a sympathising tone, a book, or a drawing, a few wild flowers, to take her in thought to hill or wood, a little fruit: this is all the poor amount of the service we can render,—but let it be paid, kindly, constantly;—let not the foot of health grow weary of treading the same path, to the same poor sufferer, week after week; and if it be so, month after month. Let us not dare to say, "I never ask for her now."

But I have wandered from my subject, and I think you will like to hear a little more of Mary D————. Whether it was that she thought she should like to see rather more of life than the farm house afforded, or whether no young farmer made his appearance just at the right time, I cannot say, but so it was, that she alone of all her sisters, stepped forth from

her father's house and began life as a mantua-maker, or rather
a general workwoman, for there was nothing she could *not*
do, from a bed tick, to a baby's cap. I said she was a *useful*
person, and so indeed she was, and her merits were soon
found out. It was, *who* should *have* her? You were obliged
to engage her weeks before, but then she remained long
wherever she went, settling the wardrobe of the whole
family for the season, and taking away with her at last, half
a dozen jobs that nobody else could do. It was in this capa-
city of workwoman, that Mary D——— at first made herself
so acceptable in our family. We children liked her to come,
because being respectably connected, and so very *quiet*, she
was privileged to sit at her work in our school room. Not
that we dared to speak to her, if we *had*, or if her presence
had occasioned the slightest interruption to our lessons, that
conscientious lady, our governess, would very soon have
effected some different arrangement; but still it was some
amusement to take a sly glance at her now and then, and to
watch the progress of our frocks, as one skirt after another
was completed, shaken out, and hung over the back of a
chair. Then sometimes too, she would quietly beckon to her
some envied child, to measure her height, (on which occasions
we drew ourselves up to the very utmost,) or to cut the pattern
of a sleeve, and then we could remind her in a whisper, of
some kind promise or other she had made us, or beg for the
little three-cornered bit of cotton print which lay near her,
and stow it away in our pocket, to be hemmed round on the
very first opportunity, for a doll's handkerchief. I think she
generally staid a fortnight or three weeks, gladly remaining
through the quiet Sunday, and partaking of the ministrations,

which she well knew how to value. It was some time though
after all this, and when we had left our pleasant village, that
on one or two occasions she proved herself to *us* as she did to
many others, a most timely and useful friend. At this time
she had pretty much given up her business of dress maker,
but she was almost always with some friend or other, making
herself useful in every possible way. Just as she was *wanted*
she seemed to *come*; and she had most extraordinary ways of
coming and going: no stage coach stopped, no bell rung; but
when, for aught we knew, she was twenty miles away, she would
be seen with her little basket on her arm, walking leisurely up
the home field, or quietly putting in her head at the open
school-room window :—but alas! as she came, so she often
went, very suddenly. I remember once she was sitting amongst
us, doing some difficult and disagreeable matters in the way
of work, which had been cunningly put by till she came, and
telling us little scraps of news concerning our old acquaintance; when the front bell rang, and an elderly farmer stopped
in a gig, or rather taxed cart, and wished to speak to her.
Poor Mary D——, she ran gaily out, but came back pale
and trembling: a friend at a distance had met with some
serious accident, and she must go directly :—so she gathered
up her work, tied on her cottage bonnet, and she was gone.

We had a sweet moonlight ride together one night, she
and I; I do not suppose I shall ever forget it. She arrived,
how it came to pass I know not, but I suppose she found out
in some extraordinary way, that *she was wanted*: but so it
was, that she arrived the very day that we had a dear little
sister born, and a very useful person she proved. Circumstances rendered it necessary to convey the little creature to

the care of a distant nurse, and *she* seemed the very person
to undertake the charge. We were very sorry the baby must
go ; the distance was fifteen or sixteen miles, and we despair-
ed of seeing it again for a long time; however, the chaise was
sent for, and the food prepared, and we knew it must be.
There were certain glances directed to *me*, and whispering
among the higher powers, which I could not comprehend, till
the pleasant announcement was made, that I was to go with
Miss D—— and the baby. Oh how glad I was ! how soon I
was ready, and how important I felt, as I sat in the chaise with
the baby on my lap, while all the several articles we were to
take, were handed in, and stowed away in the various pockets of
the carriage ; it was a December night, but mild and fine. The
moon shone clear, and as we journeyed on beneath its pleasant
light, we looked often and anxiously on the quiet features of
our little sleeping baby. How utterly defenceless it lay, how
soon probably would its life have ebbed away, without the
nourishment to which we were bearing it. I loved the little
being then, but I loved it far better afterwards. Where is
that baby now ? Oh how altered ! Intelligence has dawned
on those features, and broke upon that mind ; that wailing
voice has strengthened into the tones of strong sense, and deep
affection ; the pencil and the pen have become familiar to
those tiny hands, and those feet so helpless then, speed now
on errands of mercy to the sick and poor. And how many
are spared to mark the change ? I, who write this tale, and
she, my pleasant companion in that moonlight ride, the good
old nurse to whom we carried the babe, and he, her loving
father, who ere she went, "received her into the ark of
Christ's church, and did sign her with the sign of the cross,"

all are living yet. Oh the boundless mercy of our God! how
may we trace it in our own history, and that of those we love;
how should we delight to dwell on it, how deeply should we
feel our utter unworthiness of its daily manifestations.—
Muffle up the baby, for the chaise has stopped, and we must
run with her from the hatch, down the narrow garden path,
to Sarah's cottage. Look at Sarah, and wonder not we
brought the little one so far, to such a nurse. She is a little
old woman *now*, a widow sheltering in her son's house with
her grandchildren in her arms, and round her knees; but *then*
she was the strong active wife of the labourer, with her young
healthy boys round her, her baby in the cradle, and her helpful daughter Lyddy, ready to nurse it when it awoke from its
quiet sleep. Poor Sarah! she has had her troubles since
then: Lyddy is in the grave, and another, and another; she
is wearied and worn, and perhaps some of her happiest days
now, are those which from time to time she spends in the
house of her nurse-child.

It may chance to us perhaps, as we pass through life,
that connections or dependants in whom possibly we feel no
especial interest, come again and again, confident of a kind
reception, willing to keep up the old claim; mindful of former
kindness,—repulse them not. Let them *build* on your regard. Some small sacrifice, a little self-denial,—it needs no
more, to secure you the privilege of becoming the stay and
the comfort of some weak, and afflicted one. Poor Sarah!
Pleasant and comfortable was her cottage *then*, and as she
received the baby, and blessed it, for its parents' sake, and
took it to her bosom, we felt that it was in the place appointed, and graciously provided for it, and left it with satisfied
and thankful hearts, in that lowly home.

It was eight o'clock; very late; and I thought (heedless
of the poor horses,) that we should turn about and go home
again at once; but my companion was far more discreet;
"Now" she quietly said, we will go to supper at "Court de
Wick." "May we?" said I, thinking such a delightful
scheme barely possible, "too good news," as children say,
"to be true." However, so it really was to be. We turned
off where the base of the old cross stood, at the corner of
the road, passed along under the high wall, mantled with
ivy, drove round the moat, (for Court de Wick was a very
ancient place,) between the massive stone pillars, where was
a gateway once, and stopped before the heavy gothic door of
the old house. A hearty welcome indeed awaited us. It was
quite an adventure for a chaise to drive up there at all, especially at such an hour of a December evening. Mary D——
was welcome every where, and *I* was welcome for my parents'
sake; and then we brought pleasant news of the birth of the
expected little one; besides all which, the mistress of that
"old poetic place," was of a temper more than commonly
kind and sympathising, and kindly was the kiss she gave, and
cordial was the tone of welcome, as we entered the ample
kitchen. Her complexion is fair, and her figure light; yet
there are lines methinks in her face, that tell of nearly forty
years; and her husband, that staid and fatherly looking man,
he surely must be fifty or more,—yes, it is even so, yet look
at the white ribbon in her cap! they are bride and bridegroom.

"True lady, true, we are not girl and boy;
"Yet have we something left us to enjoy."

So wrote a true poet; and so perhaps, in substance at least,
did the substantial farmer address the fair one he had long

D

admired, when she laid in the grave the mother she would never leave. Shall I tell you more? It is a sad but a true tale. The blessing of children perhaps they scarcely expected, at any rate it was matter of wonder, and of village gossip, when their first fair little girl was born; yet another, and another came, till I believe they had five, if not six children, two of whom were girls. Then came trouble. Almost suddenly, and long before his three score years and ten, the father of that young family laid him down to die. Then, one after another, the mother laid her sons in the same grave, and looked with trembling love upon her daughters, as upon all she had left to her below.

"He builds too low who builds beneath the skies."

So indeed she learned. I know not the exact particulars; at what age, or in what disorders those fair children died; but I do know that in the aisle of our church at Y——— is a flat plain stone, recording first the father's death, and then in quick succession, that of every one of his children; and I have seen the gushing tears of that childless mother. "You did not know my eldest girl," she said. No, I did not know her, but I had heard much of her. She was one of those sweet beings, whom to look upon was to love. A month or two after her death, some friend of kind and sympathising heart, (the mother never discovered who it was,) sent her a beautiful engraving of a female head, framed and glazed, which bore a striking resemblance to her lost child. It hangs over the mantel-piece in her neat parlour, and often are her tearful eyes fixed upon it: I trust and hope that she can say with blessed confidence, "I shall go to them." *They* will not

return to *me*," seems ever present to her mind; and so deeply
has that tender heart been wounded, that she will go sorrow-
ing I believe, all her days. Well it is written, "The veil that
hides from us the future, is a veil woven by the hand of
mercy." She had no mournful anticipations when years ago
we supped so merrily with her at "Court de Wick."

But we have gone on from one event to another, and
strayed far from our pleasant village, and we must go back,
for Sally is coming to see us. She sent us a pitcher of whortle-
berries last week, and there was a letter pinned under the
cloth, that was tied down over the mouth of the pitcher.
It was folded very oddly to be sure, and sadly stained with
the juice of the whortle-berries, but there was love in the
beginning, at the end, and all through; and better even than
that, we thought; it was written large and plain, that Sally
would come on Thursday, in the wagon. Oh how much there
will be to show her! how much pleasanter for her than when
we lived in town. Sally came, and her baby in her arms;
the only one she ever had, except the infant who died. He
was a little smiling pretty fellow then; prettier and more
amusing, we children perversely thought, than our own baby
of the same age. After this he came again, and again, with
Sally to see us, and grew to be quite a favourite; and we
made him little buff waistcoats, with bright yellow buttons,
and sadly he used to cry when we parted. He lives not now,
and an abler pen than mine has told of his long illness, and
his death; and time, and quiet submission to the will of God,
and the christian's hope of a blessed immortality, have somewhat healed that deep wound in my poor Sally's heart. And
I would not write a word to tear    open, or to remind her

painfully of times and pleasures for ever past; wherefore I will pass by much respecting her poor son, which nevertheless would have been very interesting, and go back to her first visit to us at Y——.

Come! we will take her all up the village, and we shall meet a great many of our neighbours, and tell them, " this is Sally," for they have all heard of her; and perhaps we may meet some quakers riding down the road. Now I dare say it was not so great a treat to Sally to see the quakers, as it was to us; for we had never seen any, or perhaps I ought to say, never observed any, till we lived at the village of Y——. It was quite a colony of quakers, and regular old-fashioned country quakers; such broad brims, such straight bonnets; and we learned to know them all, notwithstanding the similarity of their costume. Often, as we passed up the village on our daily walk, the fair young quakers would come clustering out, with their mother at their head; and kind was their greeting, and a very pleasant adventure we always thought it. They did not venture on much intercourse; but once or twice, I remember the quaker children coming to visit us; on which occasions they were as pleased as we were, to exchange bonnets and tippets, and to play at visiting each other in the seats and bowers of our garden. There was Rebekah, what a little wild thing she was; looking up with her laughing eyes, under my straw bonnet, and tucking up the tight sleeves of her drab gown, with infinite trouble, that it might "look more in the proper fashion," as she said. Depend upon it, if that child did not greatly alter, she got "read out" long ago. But alas! these our young acquaintance, somewhat older than ourselves, early grew up into women; covered their

smooth hair with the little lawn cap, folded the clear handkerchief over their fair bosoms, and from that time became
more distant in their manner. "How dost thee do?" came
out in a graver tone, and if they called to see us, we exchanged bonnets and shawls no longer. Pleasant are my
recollections of our quaker friends. "We have not seen Mrs.
Y———— a long time," we said to her husband,—a knowing
old man, who often had a sly laugh with us. "Why no,"
said he, "our quarterly meeting is pretty near, and our women
folk, I think, make as much fuss as thine in their way; at
any rate, my Rachael has been starching and crimping for
this month, and it is not clear to me that she has done yet."
The old man was right, I fancy; you will not easily find a
better judge of a rich dove-colour silk, or a clear French lawn,
than the fair quaker. "They make as much fuss in their
way," as the grave old man said. One there was among our
acquaintance, who seemed not quite satisfied with the style of
dress adopted by her sisterhood. In fact, she ventured on
the enormity of a cottage straw-bonnet, with white ribbon
strings, and exchanged the long full cloak, for what was then
more modish, a pelisse, tied down with bows in front. I well
remember her coming one evening with Mrs. Elizabeth
G————. They staid to tea, and made some arrangements
about a flannel clothing society, to be established in the
village. Now Mrs. Elizabeth was a person of great weight;
she spoke at meeting, and discountenanced innovations of
every kind; and many a grave look did she direct towards
her neighbour, in whose costume her practised eye doubtless
discovered several slight deviations from established custom.
They rose to go; in one minute was Mrs. Elizabeth's warm
cloak put on; and what we children irreverently called her

"Pussy Cat," tied round her throat; but alas! her friend's
pelisse was a matter of more difficult arrangement, and as she
buttoned the wristbands, and fumbled at the bows in front,
and fastened the band; grave was the tone in which Mrs.
Elizabeth said, "When thou art *ready* neighbour, we will
bid our friends farewell." There was one man amused us
very much—we called him the "galloping quaker," and declared that we never looked out of the window without seeing
him riding by: he was a tall spare man with hard features,—
a grazier, and I dare say he rode about to look after his
cattle in the marshes. We felt a strange sort of interest in
the man, because we had heard that one of his great toes had
been amputated. Oh dear! children are queer creatures!
We wondered how in the world he could ride so fast without
his great toe.

Nay, but I am writing in too light a strain of so respectable a body of people. Peculiar they are certainly, but most
kind and useful.—Who more forward in works of charity and
love? Who better informed on literary subjects? Who more
skilled in useful needlework, than the "Friends?" And one I
know, whose name, might I record it, would be an honour to my
page.—I must write of her, even at the risk of wearying you,
kind reader, and I will tell of my *first*, and my *last* visit to
her. My first was more than thirty years ago, and I thought
her an old lady then. I was taken to see her, and she gave
me a little square bound book, full of pictures. It was one
of my chief treasures for many years, and I should have cared
little then, if all books had been constructed on the same
principle. I retain no other impression of *this* visit, except
an idea of the magnificence of her hall, paved with squares of

white and black marble, and ornamented with two white marble slabs, supported by gilded dolphins. The dolphins are still there, but the gilding is somewhat tarnished ; neither does the hall appear to me so spacious; yet all is handsome and suited to her station. When last I visited her, I gave a *gentle* rap, for I knew she was aged, and infirm, and when the door was opened, it was a well-known face on which I looked.

We call it a changing world, and so it is, yet some things in it last on from year to year, till we can scarcely fancy them other than they are. It has happened to me more than once, to take a kindly leave of some old lady, and travel to the other extremity of the kingdom ; and stay away months, aye *years*, and return again; and the same friend has gone with me to the door, and the same faithful domestic has opened it, and I have seen my old friend in the very spot where I left her, and looking as if she had been there ever since.

Thus it was now,—and yet there was a difference too,—The old servant did not as heretofore introduce me at once into the room where her mistress sat. "She is quite well," she said, in answer to my enquiries, "but she gets very old, and her memory fails her a *little at times*, (how tenderly she touched the infirmities of age!) and she would just tell her I was there." She shewed me into a side parlour, but I had scarcely looked round at the prints; one on two scripture subjects, and "The Quaker Family," (the placid mother and her baby, and those prim respectable gentlemen) by West; —when she came in and said, her mistress would be very

glad to see me. Oh! I knew she would—she had ever welcomed me for my parents' sake, and for the sake of some old
neighbours of hers, who had an interest in me. There she
sat, much as I had ever seen her, her small spare form hab-
ited in a rich brown silk, a fine Norwich shawl over her
shoulders; the delicate mittens drawn over her small hands;
the satin ribbon confining the border of her snowy cap. How
kindly she welcomed me! how pleasantly alluded to the
many months that had passed, since she saw me last, and,
—give her time,—her memory fails especially in *names*;—but
she will recollect presently, and enquire particularly for all
connections and relations,—for it is manifest that she is thinking not of herself, but of *you*,—*your* friends, *your* prospects.
—Then she admired the border of my muslin shawl, (the
work of that very sister, by the way, whom we left at Sarah's
cottage) and said, I was always neat;—no slight praise from
such a quarter;—and better than all this, she entered upon
*heavenly* themes; in simple but fervent language, set forth
the Christian's hope, and you felt that she was *waiting* for
her Lord, ready when he should knock, (and speedy, probably,
and gentle would that summons be,) ready to open to Him
immediately. Just look at her table; not in the massive
style of modern furniture, but a small oval table inlaid with
a narrow border of satin wood round the edge; highly
polished to the very extremity of its slender legs. There lie
her spectacles, and a little bright bunch of keys, and her
knitting; and there are her books, and a folded paper or
two,—reports of various societies, and schools; for in many
a list of subscribers to such, will you find her name. Her
ideas on such subjects are very liberal. "They all try to do
good," she says pleasantly, "and I like to help them all a

little." Her books are devotional,—old books mostly, and in a large clear type, and her Bible is ever near.—And there lies our Book of Common Prayer;—I marvel not, for I recollect an anecdote told me of her by a mutual friend many years ago. Her husband was living then, and our friend called on them on some errand of charity. They laid down a book as he entered, and as his quick eye followed it, the lively lady said, with a smile, "Aye, it *is* thy Common Prayer Book," and playfully putting her finger to her lips, added, " And I will tell thee a secret, we think it the next book to the Bible." Her husband,—but I spare you, or we shall never get on to the end of our village, and to Cadbury Hill.

"Look Sally, at that pretty garden." "Garden my dear?" said Sally, "why there is not a bit of earth." No there is not a bit of earth, at least we cannot see any ; the whole court is paved with broad flag-stones; but look at the wide crevices between them, and the cracks in the old stones,—and look at the flowers ! tall persicarias with their drooping crimson flowers, and broad leaves; blue larkspurs; marigolds of every shade, from lemon colour, to the deepest orange; lupines, and gay edging stock ; see they all spring up year after year, between the stones, and how curious and beautiful it looks. How I love *old fashioned* flowers : sweet peas, and lupines, wall flowers, and mignonette; blossoms that vary not in their character, but come year by year the same ; reminding us of the pleasant sunny nooks, where we saw them growing first. *Spring* flowers too, how I love *them*; flowers that come *only* in the spring. If the season is mild, you may find in November even, a stray wall flower, or polyanthus in the garden ; or a weakly primrose in the hedge ; but the snow drop and

crocus in the neat border, and the violet on the sunny bank ;
if you find these, *it must* be spring.  And talking of violets,
here we are, in the beautiful lane where we find so many ;
white violets mostly, and such large ones, and so sweet.  I
always think of that lane when I see a bunch of violets: the
green moss, and the snail-shells, brown and yellow, that we
picked up there, and the sprays of blackthorn, leafless, but
studded with their delicate blossoms; all is present to my
mind.  Long years after this, in the crowded market of the
neighbouring city, I would seek out the neat farmers' wives,
who came from our village, and its neighbourhood ; and as I
purchased their sweet violets, could almost fancy I knew the
very lanes where they had been gathered.  How pleasantly
in the very heart of the city, and on its busiest day, does the
farmer's wife in her accustomed place, remind you of country
scenes!  There she stands, with her various goods nicely
arranged ; the fowls so white and plump, the snowy pail with
its store of butter, each delicate half-pound wrapped round
with the cool dock leaf; the eggs, the cream-cheese, the large
red apples, and the *violets*.  Who will buy them?  A penny
a bunch!  Surely they are worth it for the memories they
bring; besides, as the mother pleasantly observes, "It is the
children's money."  In the grey twilight along the quiet hedge-
rows , they went plucking one after another, till the early
evening closed in, and they hastened home with the treasure.
Who will buy them?  Some mother perhaps will take a bunch
of them to her sick child, and in her quiet chamber help those
weak hands to arrange them in the glass.  Some young
sempstress will come, she and her companions were wondering
yesterday as they bent over their weary work, wondering
whether the *violets* were come ; and she is planning a kind

surprise by taking them a bunch. Here comes a smart foot-
man ; *his* mistress *fancies* some violets, and she will place
them on her elegant chiffonnier, in the opal vase, beside the
Indian box, and amid the gay confusion of cut glass, and
embroidery.

We thought little of all this, when we went with Sally
through that pleasant lane; now through this field and copse,
up this little steep, where on the old grey wall which bounds it,
grow such curious round fleshy leaves, and such delicate fern,
and we are on Cadbury, the beautiful hill, which formed
almost our daily walk, yet of which we never tired. Look
around at the scattered villages, all down that fertile valley !
Look at the gentlemen's seats amid the woods; there is one
quite in the distance on an eminence. I must tell my young
readers, (for perhaps they are beginning to think me rather
grave,) I must tell them a funny story we used to hear in
connexion with that house. Its master was a kindly man,
and a good landlord; and on one occasion he asked one of
his substantial tenants, why he had never brought his wife to
the lodge. He should like, he kindly said, to shew her the
house and grounds. There was much to shew, for it was the
abode of wealth and taste. Well, the farmer and his wife
came ; she was a worthy woman, I dare say, but she wanted
that quiet good sense which teaches us that we are most
estimable, and most esteemed, when we step not out of our
proper character; when we aim not at the dress or appearance
which we have no right to assume. She decked herself out
very gaily; her old husband hardly knew her, and as the
event proved, she literally did not *know herself*; for as they
entered a long gallery, terminating with a large looking-glass,

she made a low courtsey to her own figure reflected in it ;
mistaking herself for the mistress of the house advancing, as
she supposed, to welcome her: "Madam, I suppose," said she,
and long was the story remembered against the poor farmer's
wife.

——There is the village next to our own, with its pretty
white spire, and parsonage-house and garden, close to the
church. It looks well at this distance, but it is not near so
pretty as ours: it looks more like a country town. There is
an old cross, to be sure, near the bridge, but it is surrounded
and nearly blocked up, by many very poor cottages ; nevertheless we were very fond of a walk to C——y: there was a far
better shop there than our own village boasted, and it was
quite an event to have an early dinner, and join some of our
neighbours in a visit to this shop. It was kept by some of
our Quaker friends, but nevertheless, a dark green or crimson
ribbon for our bonnets in Autumn, or a pretty cotton for our
Spring frocks might often be procured there. It was a pretty
walk ; through the meadows, over a wooden bridge, just
narrow and ricketty enough to make the crossing it a matter
of interest; along the marshy field, where grew the yellow
iris and the willow herb ; and over the last high gate into
the open road. Then, ten to one, in our way home, we called
at the parsonage, where we were ever welcome ; or at the
elegant cottage of two maiden ladies, whose parlour with its
pretty trellised paper, and small Gothic windows, opened so
pleasantly on their neat lawn.

It is a beautiful view, certainly, from the old hill. There
is Cleve's Toot !—that precipitous hill crowned with its rough

craggy rock : I have often wished to ascend it, but I never
did. I remember going there once as a child, dining in the
field below, and some of the party ascending the steep Toot;
but I remained below, willingly, I hope, with one whose
slightest wish it was my duty to comply with. She said, I
had better not,—and we sat quietly in the shade, she and I,
that summer's day, till the rest of the party returned again.
" You had better not," from a mother's lips, dear children,
should ever be enough.

Look away now, Sally, towards the channel; yes, just
about there must be the beautiful village where we went to
lodge last summer. Ah that *last* summer is long past now!
and many a *last* summer has been referred to since—and that
village—how it is altered ! Really in some places the hand of
man works such a transformation, that you look bewildered
round, vainly trying to recollect how some favourite spot
looked once. It was so when I lately visited C———. Till I
got away to the old hills and the rabbit warren ; till from the
high jutting cliffs I looked down upon the dark rough beach;
and gazed on the mighty works that man *cannot* alter;—I
could scarcely believe that I was treading the same ground as
in the days of my childhood ; and when I passed along by
the straight rows of lodging houses, and saw the marine li-
brary, the new church, (the redeeming feature in the scene)
and the hotels ; and the patient donkeys in long rows with
their little white *aprons*, waiting for their young riders, and
the old gentlemen and ladies in their Bath chairs, I could
scarcely realize the fact, that in *my young* days, our old
friend Mrs. W———'s cottage was the only lodging-house in
the place ; and our arrival at it for a sojourn of six weeks,

matter of village talk and gossip. That kind friendly woman
Mrs. W——! Oh well I recollect the delight with which we
took possession of her pretty countrified parlour. A primitive place it was, low pitched, and with a heavy beam across
the ceiling; a stone floor, but partially covered with carpet-
ting, and a high plain mantelpiece. The large open fire-
place was filled with the drooping branches of the feathery
asparagus, with its pretty crimson berries;—a few pictures in
square and oval frames, a handsome old clock, and an im-
mense ostrich egg suspended from the ceiling near the window, completed the simple decorations of the room: but we
were abundantly satisfied. Mrs. W——'s very first act, was
a most kind and thoughtful one, for though "it was not in
the bond," inasmuch as she had engaged only to *lodge* us,
she had provided against our arrival a large seasoned pie,
"The little dears would be hungry," she said, "coming so
many miles, she knew pretty well what children were." She
might well say so, for she was the village school-mistress;
and in a large airy room in the yard behind her house, she
successively taught the children of three generations. Reading, and plain sewing; with the first rules of arithmetic, and
writing, for another penny a week—such was what she pro-
fessed to teach the children of the labourers and simple
farmers round; and I doubt, I very much doubt, if modern
alterations are improvements, and if there come forth now
from our *national* and infant schools, (excellent as in many
respects they are) a race of young people better conducted,
or fitter for the stations they are to occupy:—but perhaps I
am getting out of my depth.—Across the road, and bounded
by a low wall, and pretty white gate, Mrs. W—— had an
orchard, where we ran about, or sat in the shade, making

long daisy chains. One day she came into the parlour with
her apron full of large yellow apples for us, and looking very
cunningly at me, she said she had something in her pocket I
should like better still; and true enough it was, for among
the long grass in the orchard, she had found my silver thimble, the loss of which I had been lamenting for two days.
Of course I had been reproved for my carelessness; and besides, it was no trifle to lose my thimble where no other
could be procured. There were then no pretty white or "or-
moulu" thimbles, with mottos round them too, neat and
shapely and three for a penny! The young sempstress *then*,
was either happy in the possession of a silver thimble, at the
cost of eighteen pence, or two shillings; or was obliged to
content herself with a brass one of most awkward shape, too
small at the top, and too large at the bottom, and leaving an
unsightly green stain upon the finger. No wonder then I
have never forgotten the great difficulty out of which kind
Mrs. W——— helped me.

During our stay at this delightful spot, we were more
than once kindly received by the great man of the place, the
occupant of a very beautiful seat in the immediate neighbourhood. Of the house I remember little, except indeed a
wainscotted hall, an open fire place, and, perched on the high
mantel-piece above, a stuffed peacock, with its gorgeous
spreading tail;—but I have a far more distinct recollection of
the beautiful garden, reaching away from terrace to terrace,
till you had imperceptibly gained the hill-side, and stepped
out on the mossy path which leading on from one shady seat
to another, brought you in view of the wide channel, the flat,
and steep Holms, and the far coast of Wales. I well remember

the youngest daughter of this house; a little my senior I think
she was; at any rate, she was taller, and her manners probably
more formed. Great friends we were for the time, but my
kind and wise parents thought it as well perhaps, that it was
likely to be but for a time. Lasting and disinterested friendship, is not very likely to subsist between children in different
stations of life: even in our short intercourse I recollect being
much disturbed in mind, while we dressed the large wax doll.
I had cunningly chosen to be the mother, (she politely yielding
me the choice,) that I might select from her abundant wardrobe, the dress in which the doll should appear; but my
companion affirmed, that the choice rested with her, as
nursemaid; because *her* maid always chose what *she* should
wear. I suppose the affair terminated without an actual
dispute: but at any rate, I know I was sadly envious of her
as the possessor of such a beautiful doll.

How I love to see a little girl nursing her doll, singing
it to sleep, and talking to it? And how fond they are of them,
how resentful of any slight cast on them, how they cherish
them even in decay! It is a fruitful subject this of dolls,
but rather a trivial one; therefore if any little girl, or perhaps
I should say *young lady*, is reading my book, who professes
to have " Quite done with her dolls," and who now calls them
" *the creatures;*" perhaps she had better skip a page or two
till we get beyond these dolls. I knew a little thing with a
wretched old doll; she was so little, that she dragged it about
by the neck, clasping her little dimpled hand tight round its
throat; its long dirty frock dragging on the ground behind.
A most unmotherly procedure certainly—and the doll! it had
lost its wig; one eye was knocked in, and rattled about in its

head; its lips were quite kissed away, and where the arms were once, the frock sleeves hung loosely down. Yet still the little thing loved her dolly, or, as she chose to call it, her "*ittle tild*." In pure shame at seeing such a wretched thing about, I bought her a new one; and though pleased for a time with its gay frock, and sash, she was by no means willing to relinquish her old favourite. "Which of your children do you love best my dear?" I said, as she walked round and round with a doll in each hand. She looked first at one, then at the other, then at the first again, and kissing the poor dismembered doll, replied, "Think I love her best, 'cause she's so very poorly." Now what was this but the very same feeling which wakes in the mother's heart, when though she rejoices in the healthful and happy children with which God has blessed her, she turns with a more tender feeling still to the afflicted one; and lavishes on the weak, either in mind or body, her tenderest cares, and her warmest love.

But I know not how to apologise for this long digression. Sorry we were, when Sally's visit ended, and she and her little son went home again. She faithfully promised to write us a letter, and said "George would be sure to call when he came up to Fair." Now it strikes me that I have not given this respectable person that conspicuous place on my page, which he certainly deserves. We had forgiven him for being a blacksmith, when we found how good a husband he was to Sally; in fact he looked far more like a respectable farmer, when he came year by year in his excellent suit of clothes, and with that satisfied expression of countenance, which told he was "well to do," to make his purchases of iron. He was a tall stout man with a most good-tempered

E

look; and when we heard George was come, down we would
run, tumbling one over the other, mindful both of Sally, and
of certain large parcels of sugar plums, which George was
sure to have in his capacious pockets. Then the cold meat
was to be produced, and I was to mix him some spirit and
water. Now George was a very moderate man;—but still I
have thought since, that he must have found the potations I
ignorantly prepared for him, exceedingly weak.—However
he always seemed pleased and satisfied. Poor man! we
really worried him with our reiterated praises of Sally. Year
after year it was the same story; we told him of Sally's virtues, and how good a wife she was, till he really seemed to
think the balance was scarcely held with an even hand, and on
one occasion he was obliged to speak up for himself:—"Why
yes, Miss," said George, "Sally is all very well, I don't say
but she's a very good wife; and I'm thinking too that she
have a got a pretty good husband."

It was pleasant on these occasions to see Sally's master
come down to speak to George, to enquire kindly into his
circumstances; (for he was consulted in their money matters)
and to hear in their conference, words of wisdom and en-
couragement on the one hand; and of honest gratitude and
respect on the other. I must not omit the mention of one
thing for which our blacksmith was famous. His reputation
in his village was very great as a *tooth-drawer*, and (I trust
no nervous lady's eye is on my page) he drew them with *an
old pair of nut-crackers*. Sally, on one of her visits, in the
plenitude of her affection, and her anxiety to afford her
husband every advantage in his *profession*, purchased for
him some more suitable instrument. He was very thankful

to her, and thought to do wonders with it—but alas! on the
very first experiment, he failed; and throwing the new tool
aside, he said "No Sally, 'twont do;—there's nothing like
the old nut-crackers." Sally used to tell us of Mrs. Some-
body, I forget her name, but a person of some consequence
in the place, the flourishing mother of many children, and
about to add to their number; who in all the agonies of the
tooth-ache, had recourse to George and his nut crackers:—
but George was a wary man; it was a ticklish case; and he
would have nothing to do in the business, without the consent
of the lady's husband; so she was obliged to wait patiently,
till the lad, despatched for the purpose, returned with his
permission; "and then, my dear," said Sally, exultingly,
" she sat down, and George had it out in a minute, as clean
as any doctor." What the parish would do without George
and Sally, I do not know; for she is quite the doctress of the
place, very knowing in herbs, and skilled, (as may be supposed,) in the complaints of children. Indeed in every way,
she is a most kind and useful neighbour. Some few articles
of common use, needles, pins, tapes, &c., she is obliged, in
self defence, to *sell;* for her neighbours soon found out the
careful person who always had these useful articles at hand,
and "There was no end to their borrowing and begging;"
so Sally increased her stock, and, as she says, though she
does not "make much," it is not *all loss*, as it was before.

But I will not wear you out, kind reader, as we did
George, with Sally's praise.—We will change the subject. I
think the event of most consequence which occurred during
our residence at Y——, was the arrival in England of our
Grandmama; not the old friend, of course, whom we called

by that familiar name, at the Farm; but our *real* Grandmama,—our dear father's own mother.  We had never seen
her, for her life had been passed in a distant land; but she
had nevertheless made herself known to her dear little girls
in England, as she called us, by many kind remembrances.
The bright shells from her island shores, the rich sweetmeats
of Guava, and Limes, and, on one occasion I remember, some
beautiful pockets of blue and pink silk,—these, together with
long letters written purposely for our perusal, in a clear,
large hand-writing,—all came from our good Grandmama;—
so that she had established herself in our affections, long
before the well remembered summer-day, when the carriage
stopped at our garden-gate; when the son from whom she
had been so long separated, welcomed her with dutiful regard,
to his pleasant home; and the glad children were summoned
from their distant school-room to see their Grandmama.  Her
figure was very small,—she was exceedingly neat in her person, but care, (for she had had heavy trials,) and an ener-
vating climate, made her look older than she really was;—
this very circumstance however, and her extreme feebleness,
bespoke at once our *reverence*; and her gentle kindness soon
won our *love*.  Dear old lady! I am sure she deserved all the
kind attention we could pay; for though doubtless it was a
delight to her to find herself with the children and grandchildren she loved so well, and had so ardently longed to see;
—yet in her feeble state of health, it must have required a
considerable effort to undertake such a voyage; and it must
have involved no slight sacrifice of old habits, and associations, to leave the sunny Island which had been her home
so long.—To leave it too *for ever*; for I do not think she
ever contemplated a return to it, though she used often to

tell us, how many an old friend would hasten down to welcome her, should a returning vessel bear her to that shore
again. I readily believe it must have been in mournful mood,
that her eye rested for the last time on the soft and cultivated
Vale of Basseterre, rich with its cane fields, and its lofty
palms; and on the cloud-capped mountain of her lovely
island. It was not her native place, but she had lived there
long, and was familiar with its scenes and its productions.
She would tell us of its birds, and shells; its fish, and its
rich fruits; the bread-fruit tree, and the custard-apple. Much
more she would have told us, of scenery and manners, had
*we* heedless children cared to hear; and often have I regret-
ted since, that I lost the opportunity (not to return again) of
being made more intimately acquainted with an island which
became, in more thoughtful years, an object of much interest
to me. Accustomed to swarthier skins, I believe dear grandmama thought her little group of English children, " exceed-
ing fair," and in her visits to us from time to time, we were
objects of her pride, as well as her love, as we grew up into
womanhood.

Her visits to us were always paid in the summer;—in
the *warm* summer; for she shrunk from the cold, to which
she had been so little accustomed. Though feeble and infirm,
she had nothing of the listlessness often induced by a residence in a sultry climate.—She began her quiet but busy
day, at six in the morning, passing its first hours in reading
and prayer. Worldly lore she had done with :—" No, my
son," she would say, " let me read your *good* books": and
she *did* read them to the comfort of her soul. And richly
were bestowed on that christian lady, those fruits of the

spirit, " love, joy, peace, long-suffering, gentleness, good-
ness." She loved to work for us, and would sit unwearied,
hour by hour, in the quiet parlour, engaged on the plain substantial garments, of which in so large a family, a supply was
constantly needed. But she loved to be *directed* in her work,
for her meek and humble spirit ever led her to be distrustful
of herself; " You must cut it, my child, and pin it," she would
say, and then, when she had felt her ground, and was sure
she should do right, her weak but willing hands again began
their task. She could do but little by candlelight, but would
sit patiently by, at a distance from the light, pleased with the
busy scene around her; ever ready with a kind and gentle
word, and most grateful for any attention shewn her. The
short walk to and from church, and a slow turn or two on
our lawn, was as much as she could accomplish in the way of
exercise.—Again and again, on these latter occasions, would
she tell us of the absent and the dead ; of the land she had
left; and sometimes of the home to which she was aspiring.
Do I linger on my subject too long ? Oh I love such memories, and they are profitable. Of *some* lost ones we *cannot*
write; beautiful would their example be; and a life of love
would furnish abundant recollections. But it may not be ;—
in our hours of solitude they are unforgotten—in our dreams
they are too vividly present :—on our knees we pray to live
as they lived, and to die their death—but we *write* not of
*them* ; of the dearest,—the tie is too near, our grief too
heartfelt.

Shall I tell you of one of the pleasantest things that
happened to us as children, a visit to the city where we formerly resided ? We had left it with delight for the country ;

neither should we by any means have liked the idea of residing there again; but to go for a day, was quite another matter; and happy was the child whose turn it was to enjoy so great a treat. Our village could boast neither coach, nor caravan; but there was a something between both, which used to come rumbling down from the neighbouring village of C——y; and when the day (a Wednesday or a Friday,) was fixed, and two, or perhaps three places secured, how anxious we were for a fine day! how much on the alert, as we hastily took our early breakfast, and posted ourselves at the garden gate, looking up the village to catch the first sight and sound of the coach; and how full of glee we ran in, to give notice of its approach. Then there was the setting off, the importance bestowed by some penny or two-penny commission we had to execute: the nosegay of fresh flowers to be most carefully conveyed; but alas! drooping and fading with every mile of our journey. At first, probably, the coach was not very full; we could give abundant room to the clean frock, which we were anxious to preserve in all its freshness; and could lay our basket or bag, and our nosegay, on the seat at our side; but the case was different as we proceeded:—at one village we took up some nice respectable old farmer; at another a very fat old lady, and her dog; now two smart young sisters; till as we approached the city, we became full *inside* and *out*. The *child* of the party was obliged to compress herself into a very small space, or even to stand; and the whole party were well pleased when the coach stopped at the accustomed Inn, at the entrance of the city; and the passengers stepping out, gave themselves a shake, secured their respective bags, parasols, &c.; and giving a hint to the civil coachman to wait for them if they *should* be five minutes behind-hand in the afternoon, set off well pleased on their respective errands.

At this time our kind friends at the Farm were but little there. They grew old and infirm, and a city residence suited them better; and to their house our steps were always directed in the first place. Kind was our welcome,—but we were important people on those busy days. We could stay no-where very long, so the flowers were put in water; the hour for dinner was fixed; *late* it was to be, that we might do all our errands, and enjoy the last hour there, and then away we went. Stockings and shoes, summer bonnets and frocks; books and pencils, knives and scissors, maps and toys; I cannot tell you what we bought, or where we went. Parcel after parcel was sent to the Inn; enough, we thought, to fill the coach: till at length the faithful watch told us the morning was gone, and we had but a brief ten minutes in which to hurry back to dinner.

Children love variety, and there was a charm to us in the *small* dining table, with its very neat arrangements; and we lingered well pleased after dinner, over the orange, and the cake, and (must I tell the truth?) over the small glass of Noyau and water, (there were no temperance-societies then,) till there remained but just time to reach the coach. A brief but kind farewell, and away we went; ascertained that all our parcels were arrived;—stepped into the coach rather tired, and very sorry the day was over; and longed to be at home to relate our adventures and display our purchases.

Our pleasures and treats in those happy days of childhood, were very simple, but we had many of them. In fact, very little matters are sufficient to please children who are simply brought up. I have known a dear single-hearted child, look back for weeks to some particular time, and refer to it as that happy morning.—And what had she done?—She had put some plain cake, and an apple or two, into her basket; and with one companion only, had wandered far into the quiet fields:—she had found the scarlet pimpernel, or the delicate eyebright; she had brought home a wreath of briony, with its berries of green and scarlet, and yellow, and she was satisfied. I have seen two children (when dinner was ended) looking with intense anxiety towards the door,—scarcely able to restrain their merry laughter: aud what was coming? a dish of blackberries gathered in their morning walk: a surprise to their friends at home; an important secret, not to be divulged but in the exact time and place. Oh yes! children *simply* brought up, are easily pleased;—but once introduce them to more exciting things; take them to the children's ball, set them down to a game of cards, and the charm is broken.—You rob them of that which you can never restore. You teach them that which they can never unlearn. As Caroline Fry says, "I know it for I have seen it."

Certainly, as children we were rather dissipated; we were exceedingly fond of going out to tea; and I verily believe, when Joe Thomas's house was on fire, our sorrow for the poor man, was merged in the delight we felt at being packed off to a friendly neighbour's to tea, that we might be out of the smoke and dirt. Yet we were a little sorry too, to leave the exciting scene. Nothing intervened between us and the cottage, and from our school-room window, we watched with interest the blazing thatch. Our stone house with its slated roof was in little danger perhaps, but our

barn was thatched, and all hands were busy, (some, little
used to such labour) in pumping water, and pouring it on
the thatch, and on the carpets which had been hastily thrown
over it. In the mean time, our yard was filling fast with the
poor cottager's goods:—all his worldly store brought for
safety into his kind pastor's premises:—but it was no place for
children, and we went off with our governess to drink tea at
a noble old house near the church;—the rectory, in fact;—
but long occupied by one of the principal farmers in the
place. We were very fond of going there. The kind mistress of the house was always cheerful, and pleasant; and her
children were the only companions the place afforded us,
(except indeed the little quakers): then it was a curious old
place; the Gothic archway of the ample porch;—the large
and lofty kitchen, or rather hall; the parlour, with its high
narrow windows;—and up-stairs, the long galleries and
windings; all interested us; and we delighted to run about
in the garden, and orchard; and then gather round the large
table at tea-time; or try how many could sit at a time on
the "settle," a piece of furniture much in keeping with the
arrangements of a farm-house, but perhaps (such are modern
innovations) obsolete now even *there*. One seat there was we
liked better still than the *settle*; a little low form, close to
the blazing logs of wood, quite *in* the ample chimney place—
we could sit there, and look up the wide chimney, and actually see the sky at the top.—It was forbidden ground though,
and dangerous, and dirty, of course, it was; but I am afraid
we liked it all the better. A young lad too at this farm-
house used to amuse us very much;—a fat sturdy boy of
fourteen or fifteen;—very knowing already in sheep and
bullocks—coming in from the fields in his shirt sleeves, or

gaberdine, and (little observant of the refinements of society)
taking his favoured place near the lady of the house. We
were the more struck perhaps, with the manners and appearance of the young grazier, from the contrast between him and
the only youth besides, whom we ever saw at this time; a
young relative who passed his holidays with us, delicately
nice in his person, susceptible in temper,—one of the finished
gentlemen that nature makes.

Although we had few companions immediately in our
village; we had some very pleasant ones at the distance of a
few miles. The house and grounds of H———, were the
property of a gentleman residing on his estate there—the
father of a young and somewhat numerous family. It was
too far to walk,—always a delightful thing to children, for
they like riding, though they little care how. A coach and
four would not have pleased us better than James and the
cart;—indeed, I think not so much, because we should not
have been so long upon the road. Any thing however would
have been acceptable, in which we could journey to H———.
We well loved our young companions there, and we loved
their gentle mother,—and then we remained all night; sometimes indeed, longer still—and there was a bustle, and a con-
triving, and a packing, of two or three children into one bed
—in short, a *change*, which was very delightful to us. The
family was large; there were two nieces, older than the
children of the family, and besides the servants, there was old
Becky; a faithful good old woman, who had lived all her life
with different branches of the family; and though past all
labour, was to end her days here; a welcome guest in nursery, kitchen, or school-room, as she liked best. The children

of the family were very lovely; noble in disposition, and
beautiful in their persons. They were brought up in the fear
and love of God; taught to look beyond this present world,
and to fix their thoughts and hopes above. "And so it came
to pass that they escaped all safe to land." Beautifully may
the verse be applied to those who have been separated and
scattered here below. "All safe to land"! All the blooming
children who sat once round the same board; who sported
on the same turf; whose slumbers were watched by the same
mother,—but who in after life, were divided by sea and land;
tossed, some more, some less roughly, on the waves of "this
troublesome world"; how soothing to believe that all may
escape safe to land! So that gentle mother thought, and believed, when in after life she had to part with one and another
of her fair children; when trouble came upon them; when in
early life a grave was prepared for *one* in the distant Isle of
Sicily; and *another* hid her fair tresses under the mourning
cap of the widow. Poor Fanny! it needed all the mother's
faith and trust, to say "Thy will be done," when she thought
of her exiled child. She was the eldest; and we thought she
twined the closest round the mother's heart. It might be so,
perhaps. I remember once, when we were at H———,
Fanny was not there; she had gone the day before, I think,
on a visit to relatives in a distant county. Her cup was
brought in at dinner-time among the rest, and the ready tear
sprung into the mother's eye as it rested on the name. "Pardon me" she said to our governess with a sweet smile, "I am
like Jacob, *bereaved* of my child." Oh what must she have
felt in after times, when she was indeed *bereaved*; when year
passed after year, and her absent child returned no more;
when at length disappointed hope, and an unhealthy climate,

had done their work on that fair form; and with past scenes, and absent friends, in her thoughts by day, and in her dreams by night, "the cherished of so many hearts," died, alone, in a distant land. Poor Fanny! when we look back on the companions of our childhood, and follow out the history of one and another; and mark how sickness can blight, and sorrow fade; how thankfully do we turn to higher hopes, and unfading joys, and an inheritance beyond the skies.

But perhaps dear *children*, (for I feel as I proceed, that my simple pages will suit you best,) perhaps you expected something rather less grave, when I began the account of our pleasant visits to H———. Certainly there was very little that was grave connected with them then. There was some little attempt at reading, or reciting, immediately after breakfast. We were told we should enjoy our play the more, but *we* did not think so; and indeed we were very soon dismissed, and allowed to run races in the orchard, or ride round the field, two or three at a time, on the old donkey. I think we enjoyed our visits to H——— the more, because there were so many dogs and horses, and above all this same donkey. Our kind parents soon after procured us a donkey of our own, and a great source of enjoyment it proved; but otherwise we had only our two *cows*, and "Pleasant," and *a cat*. By the way, I think I know a story about a cat, that will amuse you very much. It happened though, after we had left the village of Y———, but that is not of much consequence. We had two cats; one a beauty, and a favourite; getting a little old and grave, she was; mostly a parlour guest, and in fact, rather an important member of the family;—the other a wild troublesome young thing, an interloper,—she would

*come* we knew not how, or from whence, and she would *stay*;
for on this point cats are apt to be very pertinacious. We
did not quite like to have the poor creature hung, or drowned;
so we set forth the case to our "Ironer," and descanted on the
merits of the cat; and she, kind hearted woman, (though I
believe, in her heart she would rather have been excused,)
consented to accept the cat, and take her home with her in
the evening; and as she lived in the city, three miles off, we
hoped the scheme would answer, and that we should get rid
of our unwelcome inmate. The ironer finished her day's work,
(as ironers do,) and went away. But a dreadful discovery
awaited us the next morning; we called our favourite cat,
our *beauty*, with her sleek grey mottled coat, to her breakfast
in the parlour, and she could not be found. The ironer had
taken the *wrong* cat! Now there would have been nothing
so dreadful in the affair, had that been all :—but we had just
been listening very complacently to a long discourse of the
maids, respecting the issue of the business; and how Mrs.
P——— had said, she did not think the cat would trouble
her long; for there was a sad set of boys living pretty near,
"graceless young *dogs*" she called them; who killed all the
*cats* they could find, and sold their skins. It was dreadful!
The man servant was despatched, (I think he went on horseback) to recover the cat; and one of us especially, who called
it *her* cat, waited his return in an agony of suspense; and
when she came, (for we got her back again,) how she looked
poor thing! In his hurry, the man had taken a flour bag,
to bring her home in; and sneezing and powdered, and half
blind, we hardly believed when first he tumbled her out of
the bag, on the school-room carpet, that we had got the
*right* cat home again after all. There was another cat, (if you

are not tired,) she belonged to a neighbour of ours, and he too wanted to be rid of her in a merciful way. He had a friend, a captain of a ship, going to the West Indies, and obtained from him a promise that he would take pussy to St. Vincent. He was as good as his word, and landed her on the Island; but she had no inclination to remain there. She took one glance at the Souffriere; thought the climate would be too warm for her constitution, and took her passage home again! And sure enough her master found her one morning, sitting in her accustomed place, on a low sunny wall, fringed with sweet-briar and southern-wood, blinking her eyes in the sunshine, watching the sparrows, and I dare say thinking in her own mind, as many travellers have done before her, that there was no place like old England after all.

We are wearing on to the end of our residence in our pretty village, and yet I have not told you one word about the club. The club, and the fair, which always took place on the first Tuesday in May, and was looked forward to, as a holiday and treat all the year round. The condition of vegetables and fruit on the first Tuesday in May, became quite a test of the backwardness or forwardness of the season; for many an old gentleman, and many a careful housewife, examined their asparagus beds, and gooseberry bushes, that the first dish of " *grass*," and the first green-gooseberry-pudding, might make its appearance on the day of the club. Friends came from a distance; smart young girls, who had gone off into service, begged for their day or two's holiday *then* ; and came back neat and trim, with a hoarded shilling or two to spend for their younger brothers and sisters at Y——— fair. Cottages were whitewashed, gardens were trimmed up; and if it was

but a fine day, our village presented a very gay scene, on the
first Tuesday in May. There were evils, doubtless, in the
system, and instances of disorder and intemperance, but they
were likely I think to be fewer in a country parish, where the
inhabitants were all known to their minister, and lived on,
year after year, under his eye, in the same cottage or little
farm,—than in cities where the number of his parishoners,
and, still more their constant migration from parish to parish,
renders it far more difficult for the shepherd of the flock to
keep the wanderers in view, and seek to lure them back to
the fold. I am willing to believe, that when the clubs assembled annually in our parish church, (though numbers entered
*then*, who came at no other time,) yet I am willing to believe,
there was among the members generally, a reverence for the
place, a love for their pastor, and a willingness to listen to
his instructions; and when from the appropriate text, "These
are *spots* in your feasts of charity," that faithful minister
set their misdeeds before them; and then in tones of persuasive eloquence exhorted them to repentance and faith, and
led them on to the glorious contemplation of " The rest that
remaineth for the people of God;" and pointed out to them
their only refuge, "the Lamb slain from the foundation of
the world." - I trust and believe that on such occasions, the
conscience was awakened, the judgment enlightened, the heart
of the trembling comforted.

It was *before* the clubs assembled for service in our
noble church, that they paraded the parish. The music told
us from a distance when they were approaching, and we ran
to the garden gate, or to the front window to see them pass;
a long procession, the men first, and the women (for there

was a woman's club too,) afterwards. I think they would
have shewn their gallantry by giving precedence to the ladies;
but perhaps their walking behind their husbands, and fathers,
was a practical lesson of submission, which did them good; at
any rate, so it was. The men had the gayest flags and cockades;
but for all that, *we* were more interested in the women's procession; there was more variety, more to be commented upon,
in the way of gowns and bonnets; and then it was a most
interesting thing to recognise old acquaintance; our own
washerwoman, or ironer, Mary Jones, or widow Clark, or old
Betty, and to see how very nice they looked in their new
gowns, and to nod to them when they looked up, as they
were sure to do, to see the young ladies. It was really a
pretty sight altogether. The women all had blue cockades
pinned on the breast, and beautiful nosegays and blue
wands. Old and young met there; connections and relations
went in friendly procession together, to the house of God;
and as one and another was missed year by year, a kindly
feeling was awakened towards those they had left behind.
Often the old and decrepid remained, and the helpful young
wife, the kind striving mother, was taken. Thus it *has* been,
and thus it *will* be.

It was while the clubs were dining in the large room of
our only Inn, (the quietest time in the day,) that we went to
the fair. A very unpretending fair it was. There were no
shows, no music, not even a little man, or a sheep with five legs,
it consisted merely of booths all up the village street; some
loaded with gingerbread and oranges, and others, more inviting
still, gay with every description of common toys. Horses,
spotted white and red, with rabbit-skin manes, and tails; little

green carts with red wheels; tin boxes in endless variety,
and twopenny, and even sixpenny dolls, swinging on a string,
all of a row, with yellow fuzzy hair, and blue glazed calico
gowns, with a patch of gilt paper in front. Yet such as our
fair was, we looked forward all the year round to the splendid
purchases we should make there: many little customers
spent their *all*, on these occasions, and I remember one little
boy, who got sadly laughed at, for spending his sixpence in
a box to keep it in. Many a little one came with mother,
or grandmother, from distant parts of the parish, and in the
happy possession of a whip, or a penny trumpet, forgot the
weary miles as they travelled home again.

The best booths I think, were clustered round about the
village Inn; and the gay flags furled up, and the blue wands
resting together in large masses against the wall of the house;
all gave interest and life to the scene. There was more space
too just here, for the Inn, a substantial building of grey stone,
lay back from the road, the space in front affording room for
several picturesque objects: the stone well, the indispensable
"upping stock," and a sort of rough branching post, name-
less, I believe, but very common in dairy counties, on which
the neat housewife hangs her snowy pails, and sieves, to dry
in the sunshine. A portly couple were the master and mistress of this well-conducted Inn; the landlord especially,
was the village wonder, for it was asserted, that ponderous as
he then was, he had been so small at his birth, that his wrist
was no bigger than his mother's thumb, and they put him
into a quart pot, and into his father's shoe, and in short, did
all those extraordinary things to the poor little animal, which
*are* done to such diminutive babies; that posterity may re-

member how exceedingly small they were. That village inn, with its stone well, reminds me of a pleasant old friend, sometimes our guest at Y———. On one occasion of his coming, it so happened that we could not give him a bed, and he slept at the inn. In the morning my father went to look after him, and bring him to breakfast with us; and there, at the well, stood his friend, in his shirt sleeves, flourishing his toothbrush in the pail of water, and ruralizing to his heart's content.—A kind and hearty and pleasant man he was,—*was*, nay *is*, for he lives yet: the widow and fatherless shelter with him, and the friendless look to him for help. Long may he be written of in the *present* tense.—Do not look grave, dear children, and anticipate a grammar lesson,—" present," and " imperfect," and " pluperfect," you think, are all very well in their proper places. Yet I must tell you, for all that, a little story, connected with your old friend Lindley Murray. A mother was explaining to a little girl, (she was *very* little) the distinction between nouns "common" and nouns "proper" and gave the word " Mother," as an instance of a common noun. Now there was something in the word " common," that the little lady did not like as connected with her mother; " I can't have you be a *common* noun," she said ; the mother smiled, and explained again ; " Well then," said the little thing, " if there *are* a great many mothers, there is not *one* so kind, and so you *shall* be a *proper* noun"; and she clapped her hands and laughed at the result of her own triumphant logic.—I thought it a pretty story,—but I am getting too discursive.

There was another gentleman, a tall, spare, grave clergyman, with a little rosette in his clerical hat, who used

sometimes to come and see us; but he was not much of a
favourite with us; we were but little in the parlour when he
came;—he was an old bachelor, and I suppose thought
children rather in the way. An old bachelor! and have I
dared to connect aught repulsive with the word; when the
very best, the very dearest guest we ever had, was an old
bachelor! and we would not have had him married for the
world; so dearly did we love him as he was. What a stir
there was when he came! the very servants were glad, and
we children flew about the house half wild with delight; for
he came from a distance, and but seldom; and we loved him
next to our father and mother. Then, when the first trans-
ports were over, how we clustered round him, and climbed
his knees two or three at a time; and made him sing all his
songs over and over again! Dear honoured guest! he was
my father's schoolfellow, and he has lived to see his friend's
children's children on his knee, and his love is unwearied yet.
He has shared our sorrows, and our joys, with true and blessed sympathy; as welcome, and it is saying much, as welcome
when the shadow of death was on our dwelling, and he followed in the train of the mourners; as when a blither voice
summoned him to the bridal, and his blessing was given almost with a father's fervency. We are told of the instability
of earthly friends, and I know we are poor weak unstable
beings, but blessed be God! there *is* friendship, nevertheless,
on which we may count; there *are* friends, of whom we feel
certain, that their love for us will cease but with their life;
but such friendship is not of earthly growth; it is found only
among those of whom we may say with St. Paul; "Ye your-
selves are taught of God to love one another."

I have not told you much of the poor people at Y——.

Their pastor knew them well, and they knew *him*, and loved
him. His gentle bearing, his affectionate remonstrances, his
liberal hand, his playful kindness to the young, were not ill
requited among his simple and respectful people. Twenty
years afterwards, the young minister at Y—— said with much
feeling,—" I *ought* to know you; in many a cottage *yet*, I
hear of your good father." *He* knew them well; but we
were too young to be of any use in the cottages of the poor;
and the grand business of our days then, was the fulfilment
of our school-room tasks, and our daily walks. Yet such
poor as lived up and down the village street, we of course
became acquainted with. There was James Chapman, a good
old man in the workhouse, who would fervently give us a
christian's blessing; and Joe Tilley, a poor old fellow who
worked on the roads, and who would so civilly scrape away
the mud, and make us a clean place to cross. In a funny
three-cornered house, the gable end forming a sort of front,
lived a good-tempered old body, who was sure to come out
to her rails to have a little bit of chat as we passed; and almost opposite to us, lived Nancy Thomas;—a fabricator of
certain half-baked gooseberry-tarts, with treacle on the top.
Happy the child who could procure one of Nancy's *halfpenny*
tarts, but a *penny* one was a treat indeed! not to be thought
of above once or twice in the season. But among the poor,
my most vivid recollection is of one Flower, or Flora Holmes.
The name suited her once, perhaps, but it seemed little to
befit the old woman, shrunken and crippled as she then was.
Yet she was neat and clean, and of a humble thankful turn;
no wonder I remember her, for duly every Sunday, at our
early dinner-hour, did I step across the road, with a plate of
warm meat and potatoes, for the poor old woman. It was

but a minute's work to place her little round table, and reach
her a knife and fork; but she was full of apologies at my
having so much trouble, and sent her humble duty for the
dinner, and hoped we should never live to want it.

It was about four years in the whole, that we lived thus
simply and happily at Y——.  Sally came again to see us,
and in the intervals of her visits to us at different times, she
and I continued to be very punctual correspondents.  I was
advanced in the art of penmanship, and would fain have
written to Sally oftener than I was allowed to; but the res-
triction was quite proper.  Very young ladies, indeed *all*
young ladies, have little idea of economising in postage.
There were other remembrances though, besides letters, which
passed between us and Sally.  My first attempt at fancy
work, was in the shape of a muslin cap to be spotted for
Sally; and as to *her*, she was ever devising some kind token
of her love to her dear young ladies.  Duly every summer
came our favourite whortle-berries, (a fine bunch or two carefully placed on the top, that we might see how they grew.)
How we loved to see the full dark berries swimming about in
our basins of milk; and with how much pleasure meditated
on the great batch of pies which was sure to follow the arrival
of Sally's pitcher.  But it was towards Christmas, that her
munificence was yet more liberally manifested,  Then came
the hamper; Oh how pleasant it was to run down when we
heard it was come, and proceed to the unpacking.  It was
no very easy matter; for Sally was famous as a packer, and
again and again had she passed the long packing-needle
through the interstices of the hamper; and tightly had she
drawn the strong cord, and our fingers ached with many a

desperate pull, before the cover was fairly lifted up. Then the little ones were told that they really must stand out of the way; and one was posted in a chair, and another was promised one of Sally's apples if she would leave the straw alone. The straw! it was quite wonderful so much straw could come out of the basket; even if it had held nothing else. But see what a couple of fowls these are! Really if that place were not famous for fowls, we should take them for turkey-poults :—and here, wrapt up so nicely in a cloth, is a piece of Sally's "*streaky* pork," as she calls it, (ah, she told us about her pig,) and look at the apples! and here, tumbling out with the straw, are the walnuts from Sally's own trees, and the wood nuts; (we know well *who* gathered *them*) I do believe the bottom of the hamper is quite full of nuts! Oh pleasant, pleasant memories of childhood! I write on, till the scene is present before me,—the scene, and those who witnessed it, and busy thoughts of the past *will* come, till the tear springs in my eye.—

> "Alas! for love, if this were all,
> "And nought beyond.—Oh Earth !"

We were sorry certainly to leave Y——. At any rate the elder ones among us. (for I was twelve years old at this time) thought that we *ought* to be sorry, but children love a change, and all the excitement of "moving house," as it is rather incorrectly called. It is when we have advanced some way in the journey of life; have fainted in the sun-beam, and shrunk from the storm; when the heights we may have reached, have not afforded the fair prospect we had anticipated, and the cloud of evening is shadowing the scene; it is en that we look back on some quiet valley, whose charms

we heeded little perhaps at the time ; and are fain to wish we
had lingered somewhat longer in its pleasant shade.

Yes, children are fond of change. I was once the inmate of a house, when, in one of the gales of wind, which I
cannot but think have been more frequent and violent of late
years than formerly; in one of these gales, and a tremendous
one it was, down came the kitchen-chimney! The tall lime-
trees were swaying and creaking in the wind, and uplifting
the earth at their roots; and the old high chimney was rocking fearfully, but these " signs of the times" were little heeded
by the lady of the house; for she happened to be very busy,
and besides that, she had a husband of a mechanical turn,
very knowing in most things, who had often pronounced of
this very chimney, (which formed matter of speculation in
every high wind) that it was all the safer for rocking.—
Nevertheless in one instant, with a fearful crash, down it
came;—damaging the back part of the house considerably
in its fall. Poor lady! I really pitied her! In her bedroom
the wall was broken through, and her neat dressing-table was
strewed with bricks and lime : in her kitchen, her custards
and orange jelly (for it so happened that preparations were
making for a party) were powdered with a heavy shower of
soot and brick-dust, and her smutty and bewildered maids,
were asking her what they had better do *first.*—And the
children,—(for there were two, a boy and girl)—they, heedless little mortals, were thinking it all very good fun ; and
quite delighted when it was pronounced, that they must all
leave the house which had been so full of comfort, and so
neat, an hour before ;—and must go into lodgings : the boy
pronounced it—jolly!—capital! and marched off, securing

nothing but a peg-top, which happened to be the rage at the time; while the little girl, delightfully busy, was begging for paper and twine, and proceeding to pack up the "numbers of things" she was sure she should want at the lodgings. And at these lodgings, confined and dingy as they were,—all was "couleur de rose" in the children's eyes; the heavy dull-looking sideboard, in the drawers of which their mother was laying some sheets of clean paper, to make them look rather more inviting;—*they* thought "a most convenient thing!" The old prints round the room, and the alabaster urns on the mantel-piece, were "beautiful." They gave not one thought, simple children, to the light and tasteful parlour they had left; its ample chimney-glass, and elegant French clock,— the book-case in its pretty recess; the side table with its bouquet of late flowers; (delicate monthly roses, snow-berries and laurestinus,) and its hyacinths thrusting down into the glass their long fibrous roots, and in their little green apex giving promise of scent and bloom. In the delightful novelty of their lodgings, little cared they for all they had left behind.

Yes, children love a change, and I have gone a long way, and taken a great deal of trouble to convince my readers that *we* were not fonder of novelty than others of our race, when we hailed a change of residence with childish satisfaction. Nevertheless we were not so heedless, but that there were times of graver thought and deeper feeling. One such occasion was the farewell sermon, from the appropriate text, "Who hath believed our report." We had sympathy enough with the kind and pleasant neighbours we were about to leave, to look on very gravely as one and another joined us in our way from church, and the silent pressure of the hand,

and the starting tear, told their heart-felt sorrow. I remember one poor boy, among the eldest in the Sunday School, (a well-conducted lad, whom his minister noticed with especial regard;) as he passed with the others, sobbing as if his heart would break. "What ails thee lad?" said the steady man who acted as schoolmaster; "Leave him to himself a little while," said the kind pastor; and as he laid his hand on the poor boy's shoulder, his tears streamed faster than before. "I cannot think what ails the lad," pursued the man, "I hav'nt said a word to him."—No ;—he *couldn't* think what ailed him. He was a worthy man, conscientious and pains-taking, but *impenetrable*; there was *that* working in the boy's mind, with which his own had no sympathy. It is so as we pass through life. There are not many who *understand* us. Many when they mark (if they *do* mark) the moistened eye, and the quivering lip, cannot think "what ails us." Some few, (treasured ones they should be,) discern what is passing within, and "leave us to ourselves a little while,"—

"Till the heart's deep well-spring is clear again."

It was exceedingly entertaining to us to see from our school-room window, which looked out upon the yard, the wagons piled with furniture; and I fear we liked the whole affair the better, from the necessary interruption to lessons and business. Our school-room was the *last* to be dismantled in the house we left, and the *first* to be set in order in the one to which we were going; nevertheless there was a sort of inter-regnum,—an interval of comparative idleness and misrule, which I am afraid was but too pleasant to us.

Many were the questions put to our man-servant, who had gone with some of the furniture, as to what sort of a place it was ; and rather curious was his description. Though within twenty miles of our village, it differed much from it in character ; and there was in the general appearance of the neighbourhood, and the costume of the inhabitants, some ground certainly for the opinion our simple James expressed ; that to his mind it was a " main outlandish place." I do not know exactly how it happened, but *I* was the first among us to see this " outlandish place ;" I mean among us children. Though a mile or two from the city, (the same we had formerly inhabited) it wanted the quiet seclusion which we had been used to connect with the idea of the country. Situated on the high road between two large cities, the approach to the house was very different from our pretty village street ; yet there was something imposing in the high gates between their massive freestone pillars ; and the house was a large and good one, though there was nothing very inviting in the straight gravelled path between a wall on one side, and a high hedge of evergreens on the other, which led up to it. The house too at this time, had a very gloomy aspect. The late incumbent had resided in it for half a century, and a widower, and childless, he had felt little inclination to do much in the way of renovation and improvement. The rooms though lofty, and of good dimensions, were rendered gloomy by the blocking up of many of the windows ; the paper-hangings were dark, and of large heavy patterns : the furniture scanty and antique ; and the house altogether wanted that wholesome and cheerful freshness, which nothing but a free admission of light and air can give. Little did I think how great a change might soon be effected in the aspect of things.

As we had *found* our house and garden at Y——, so had we *left* it;—but now the case was altogether different.

Make a *vicar* of your *curate*, and you shall soon see how much of liberal taste, and happy contrivance was latent in the mind, and only wanted opportunity to display itself. Our house soon assumed a light and pleasant aspect. Contemplating it (if such were the gracious will of God) as their abode for many years; our dear parents spared not expense, either in its fitting up or its furniture. "All very nice, all very pretty," said an elderly lady as she was kindly shewn over the house, and remarked the fresh paint, and neat papering; the new stair-carpet, and the pretty sideboard. Poor lady! we followed behind to hear and see, as children are so fond of doing; and wondered why, as she said it, she looked so very melancholy. We had not then been to *her* house, and passed through the shattered gate, and neglected garden, into the parlour with its worn carpet, and stained and damaged wainscoting: and we knew not then, that not many years had passed, since she was mistress of a house far more spacious, and more nobly furnished than the one she was surveying. Poor lady! she has long passed from her earthly home. I knew little of her, but if her removal has been to mansions that "wax not old" to "an inheritance in the heavens that changeth not"—it little matters what was the house she left below: it little matters *now*—but these things affect us *here*, and I marvel not now, as I did then, at her suppressed sigh.

In our garden, the change effected was still greater than in our house; but of course it was more gradual. In fact the entire transformation which took place there was the work of years. The straight wall and hedge were done away with.

The orchard and kitchen-garden became a part of the pleasure ground. Clematis and creeper, twined around the apple-trees which were allowed to remain, and climbed up to festoon the rough branches of the old cherry-tree; and winding paths, and bowers and shrubs, so arranged as not to interfere with peeps of the distant country, made our pleasure ground the prettiest for many a mile round. Sweet pleasant garden ground! how many dear ones have trodden its turf! what lovely little children have coursed each other down the slope, and under the deep shade of the horse-chesnut trees, have gathered up their dark brown balls; or watched the rich butterflies as they settled on the lilac blossoms of the autumn daisies. The sweet-briar walk, and the low curved brick wall, so mantled with roses and honeysuckle, and ivy, that you must take my word for it that there is a wall there; and the hydrangias in the turf, with their full blossoms lasting all through the summer months; and the jasmine, which we have loved and watched so many years. These are a few of the pleasant things in our garden. I would fain linger there yet longer—but it cannot interest other hearts as it does mine.

With respect to neighbours, and friends, in our new residence, we soon found that they would prove far fewer in number than those we had left; and we looked back with fond regret to our accustomed tea-drinkings at the farm houses. Nevertheless there were one or two families with whom we had very pleasant intercourse; and altogether our new acquaintance were far more aristocratic. Very near us, lived an old lady and gentleman who soon asked the little folks to tea. Starchy and stiff enough it was, to be sure, and we were on our very best behaviour all tea-time. The tall urn, the small oval tea-

waiter, the prim waiting-maid, and the little square bits of
buttered toast; I can see it all *now*, and moreover the little
old gentleman's "brown George" and the silver buckles in
his bright black shoes.   Glad enough we were to he dismissed
into the garden, to run races in the broad gravelled walk ; to
hide among the the shrubs, and above all, to gaze in wondering
admiration at the figure of a soldier as large as life, cut out in
wood, painted red, cheeks, and coat and all, and stuck bolt
upright at the termination of the long walk.

Far pleasanter were other visits we occasionally paid, to
a kind and pleasant family somewhat farther from us.   Num-
berless amusements did they kindly find, and *invent* for us,
and in particular, there was a large doll, not to be played with
for the world,—but it was treat enough to look at it; a large
handsome doll, dressed as the fashion was when the lady of
the house was young.   The only family which could have
afforded us companions of our own age, left the place much
about the time that our residence in it commenced.   They
came to see us once; three little pale girls in deep mourning,
and their brothers older and younger than themselves with
them.   Some *promise* of the talent and skill, which in after-
times gladdened the heart of the widowed mother, and
smoothed her path, had already manifested itself in her children; and we looked with wondering admiration, on the little
meek-looking girl, who we were told could draw such beautiful
flowers and fruit: but it must have been a time of much
anxiety with the mother of those young children.   We knew
them in after life; they had improved the talents God had
mercifully bestowed on them; and traced out for themselves
a path of honourable independence.   Some, "were not."   His

eyes who are in every place, had looked on them, and at his pleasnre "one was taken, and another left"—it is often so, he knows for what gay spirits the world will prove too alluring; for what meek and sensitive ones it will be all too rough; and again, and again in infinite mercy, sends from above and takes them.

One very simple treat we had sometimes and yet I must tell it, because connected with a very old and kind friend, our pleasant curate. He would come and fetch one and another of us to breakfast with him. The distance was but short; and his lodgings were but humble, and we had no greater dainties than a cup of coffee, and a two-penny loaf of new bread;—but it was wonderful what a treat we thought it; indeed I recollect feeling somewhat dissatisfied because he did not ask *me* as often as the others. It was a very hard case; for I do not recollect that I ever went there more than once or twice. Whether, (for though *I* gave it not a thought then, others might;) whether I really was growing too tall and womanly, to breakfast often tête a tête with the young curate; or whether he preferred the livelier prattle of my younger sisters, I cannot say; but so it was. However, I forgave him, and indeed we were very good friends afterwards.

There were many agreable things, certainly, connected with our vicarage. The moderate distance from the city, was in many respects, pleasant and convenient. Many a walk did we take there with our dear father, (for alas "Pleasant" and the pillion, were somewhat too rustic for the neighbourhood,) and ever was he pointing out objects of interest; picturesque bits; fine effects; and, lingering at his side in the print and picture shops, we early became familiar with

all his favourites; learned to admire the depth of shadow in
the "Jew Rabbi"; and the majesty of Salvator's Wilderness.
Then he had acquaintances and friends, among the professors
of an art he dearly loved; and as our native artist, Bird, produced one and another of his finished pictures, we were sure
of a kind reception at his house, and went again and again,
till we became familiar with the pretty modest bride at the
country auction, the young mother in her cottage home, or
the glorious Philippa at her husband's feet. These were ad-
vantages and pleasures which we could not have enjoyed at
Y——, and I must own besides, that though we ceased not
to regret our hearty old country friends, our proximity to the
town, gave us access to society likely to be more improving:
and then if we had lost the delights of the fair, we enjoyed
those of the tithe-dinner.

Oh I must tell you about the tithe-dinner, before I have
quite done with my early days. You will wonder perhaps,
that, as of course we young ladies did not dine with the gentlemen, there could have been any thing very pleasant about
it;—but I will enlighten you: in the first place there was a
great deal of preparation needed; and the night before, we
elder ones sat up far beyond our usual early hour; and after
supper, we all sat round the table, stoning raisins for the
magnificent plum-puddings. That dear old bachelor friend I
told you of, was many times with us on these occasions; and
he would sit by the fire, (for the tithe-dinner came late in the
year) and sing us songs one after another, and laugh with all
his heart, at some joke cracked by his old friend; and once
or twice he actually helped us stone the raisins. But the
great preparations were in the morning; and we loved the

bustle of an early dinner in the school room, and the setting-out of the very long dinner table. When once the guests were seated at it, the grand anxiety of the day was over; but there was still the punch to be made and tasted. Tea and coffee, I think, were dispensed with; and the guests dropped off one after another, at an early hour; and then came the pleasantest part of the day, when several gentlemen, old friends from the neighbouring city, who had kindly joined the party, would find us out in our cool quiet room, and relate to us all the funny things that had happened; and our old friend would slyly tell us there was not a bit of pudding left for us; so beautifully had we stoned the raisins.

Thus passed many years, till we numbered nine brothers and sisters; and the elder ones among us were growing up into womanhood. We had trials, but it pleased God that they should be few; and far, far out-numbered by his abounding mercies.

But what has become of Sally? When " the Pursuits of literature" was published, the poem was spoken of in some review, as a peg to hang the notes on. So I think Sally has been the " peg," on which I have contrived to hang a great deal of desultory matter. And yet I am something like the little girl who did not like her mother to be called a "common noun:" I do not much like to call dear Sally a " peg!" I would rather compare her in the position she holds in these pages, to the thread of gold I have seen tracing its way through the wreaths of flowers in some old piece of embroidered silk, and giving richness and value to the whole. However take which simile you will, so you let me pursue my favourite topic. And

G

now the time came, when one of my first wishes was to be gratified; that of seeing Sally in her own pretty cottage. We had friends and relations in her neighbourhood who had long wished to see us among them; and I and one of my dear sisters set off a long time ago, in the pleasant spring, on the promised visit.

Have you ever in passing a print shop, glanced at some head, and turned again, and dwelt delighted on the features, and thought it scarcely possible that so speaking a resemblance of some dear friend, should have been intended for any other? It has happened to me,—and it has happened to me too, to find in a poet's pages, a portrait unintended, but perfect in its resemblance to this my loved companion. I am glad of it; for if I wrote of her as I think, she would not like to read the page, and you, my kind reader, might think I had forgotten my promise, of telling you only truth. But the work is done for me.

"Led by an early custom Lucy spied,
" When she awaked, the Bible at her side.
" That ere she ventured on a world of care,
" She might for trials, joys or pains prepare
" For every dart a shield—a guard for every care.
" She mixed not faith with fable, but she trod
" Right onward, cautious in the ways of God.
" Nor did she dare to launch on seas unknown,
" In search of truths by some adventurer shown;
" But her own compass used, and kept a course her own.
" The one presiding feature of her mind,
" Was the pure meekness of a will resigned;

"A tender spirit, freed from all pretence
Of wit, and pleased with mild benevolence.

Again,

"Lucy loved all that grew upon the ground;
"And loveliness in all things living found.
"The gilded fly, the fern upon the wall,
"Were Nature's works, and admirable all.
"Pleased with indulgence of so cheap a kind,
"Its cheapness never discomposed her mind."

Such was my companion in that pleasant journey. We were young travellers, and exceedingly careful of our various packages, settling the smaller ones in the pockets of the coach, and requiring a reiterated assurance from the dear friends who " saw us off", that the larger ones were safely stowed on the roof, or in the boot. What a fearful thing a stage coach is, as it comes swaying from side to side, and rattling down the hills! What an amusing thing it is;—how much of character may we glean, in spite even of English reserve, from one and another passenger. Now the old traveller takes his seat.—*Old*, not in years perhaps, but in experience. He has forgotten nothing. His portmanteau is safely lodged. In his great-coat-pocket is his silk night-cap and his Bandana handkerchief; he gives one knowing and determined shake of the head, and cads and porters retire in despair. He draws from his pocket the newspaper of the day, and is just as free from all anxiety and care, as if he were sitting at his own fireside. But who springs in beside him ?—A pale intelligent-looking youth, with a boat-cloak hung across his arm: he looks anxiously round, "hopes he does not incommode,"—and he is gone. He had got into the wrong coach, poor lad! and see! he has left his cloak, and his silk handkerchief; and as a boy runs after him with them, our first traveller, who by the way, must take more notice than he appears to do,— exclaims, " Upon my word, such people deserve to *lose* their property." Then, have you not seen the little old lady? She is not going very far, and she takes care to tell you, that "she is very little used to stage coaches :" she ties the handkerchief closer round her throat, and thinks *one* of the windows had certainly better be shut, and hopes she shall get to her friend's house long before dark. But I beg your pardon, dear Lucy, at this rate *we* shall never get on.

How pleasant we are apt to think would be a *vivid* recollection of past scenes! There are generally, I think, a few such treasured up in the mind. We can sometimes, as some dear friend welcomed us, recal to mind the very place where they stood, the very dress they wore; while more frequently we retain no more than a general recollection of a kind welcome, and the greeting of a well-known voice. It is a pleasant thing to arrive at the end of a long journey. After the first kind embrace, to find all so nicely prepared in your room; and quickly laying aside your bonnet and shawl, to join your friends again at their social tea, and ask, and answer a hundred questions. Then, the next morning to rise early, (for *young* travellers must not *fancy* they are tired,) unpack, and free from all the dust of travel, in the fresh morning gown, with your work-box at your side, establish yourself in the well-known breakfast room; or run once round the dewy garden. As one and another old friend welcomes us, we may mark perhaps, what we saw not the night before, in some *young* friend, a trace of care, in some *older* one, deeper furrows, or a step less firm; for we do not part and meet again without changes such as these: but there is the old affection;—the same dear smile;—the calm temper, and cheerful spirits;—blessed fruits, we believe, of Christian charity and Christian hope.

It was a pleasant retired spot to which we went first. The situation of the house, perhaps, was not very well chosen; for in the midst of very beautiful scenery, it had been built at the bottom of an ascent; and the garden sloping upwards from the parlour windows, precluded all view but of its own fresh turf, its flower beds, and its filbert trees. But a few minutes walk took us away to the open fields, the copse, and the hill. That pretty copse, which our host shocked us by declaring should very soon be a corn field if the estate were his own. I have little to relate of this visit; for at this distance of time, its circumstances have faded from my remembrance. A pleasant memory of scenes visited in youth, and friends familiar then, is sometimes all we seem to grasp of pleasures so fleeting. Connections formed in later life, and newer scenes come between us and them; and we long in vain to see yet once again, the old familiar faces which smiled on us in the fresh days of our childhood and youth.

We had taken our sketch books with us, and in the place of our next sojourn we found abundant use for them. We were, where nature's children love to be—on the shore of the glorious sea!—among the alabaster rocks—beneath the stupendous cliffs;—treading the moist hard sand, and collecting bright shells, pink, and white, and yellow, for the little ones

at our distant home.  Little do they know of the sea as it
washes our beautiful western coast, who are familiar only
with the long lines of unbroken shingle, and the bare white
cliffs of Kent and Sussex.  Certainly there is no greater
contrast than between the solitary rocks of Ilfracombe or
Lynmouth, and the Marine Parade of Ramsgate or of
Margate.  We wandered for hours upon the beach;—but
our careful friends, an elderly lady and gentleman, saw danger where we discerned none; and would not let us go without
a little lad, professedly to carry our basket of shells and alabaster, but in reality to see that the young ladies did not get
into danger.  Nor was the caution needless; little isolated
rocks on this picturesque coast, and jutting promontories,
afforded pleasant resting places.  But fearful tales were told
of some who had lingered on such too long, and called in
vain for help, as the unsuspected tide came in, and the waves
rose higher and higher, and cut off their retreat.  It was not
to be wondered at that our kind hostess was anxious about us,
for we were dear to her, as the children of her schoolfellow,
and earliest friend; and she might well be rendered timid by
circumstances.  Her whole life had been passed in this small
fishing town; and she had witnessed many a scene of distress
on a coast where shipwreck was not unfrequent.  Very kind-
hearted, and almost the only persons in the place who were
in easy circumstances, she, and her husband were frequently
called on for kind assistance and sympathy in such cases;
and she could tell you of the fatherless children her house had
sheltered,—of the stranger lady with whom she had gone to
gaze on the features of the shipwrecked dead; and of that
poor widow's shriek of agony at the sight.  Is it any marvel
then, that she hailed us gladly, each time we returned from

the beach, and that she loved better to watch us as we
mounted the winding path up the hill to St. Decuman's
Church ?

St. Decuman, tradition says, swam across the Channel
with his head under his arm. Pity that so unlikely a circumstance is the only one I can hear or read respecting him.—
There must have been events of note, and less questionable,
in his life; and merits he must certainly have had, or this ancient and highly-decorated church would not have been dedi-
cated to him. Built long since, but earlier ruined, stands
close to the church, what was once the parsonage. The damp
walls are stained with lichen and moss, and the straggling
ivy has found its way into the very rooms,—if rooms they
may yet be called, so desolate, silent, and cold. The ruin,
perhaps, by this time, is a heap of stones; and our old friends,
they are living, but they are changed. I think of them with
grateful love, but I shall probably see them no more.

We were in a neighbourhood abounding in old friends
and old associations. During long summer visits here as
children, we had often passed through scenes of surpassing
beauty, without much heeding them. Many a little voice, at
the usual boundary of our daily ride, exclaimed, "I spy Dun-
ster Castle first,—for it was an object that even children
could not pass unnoticed. I would that my powers of description were less limited, that I might bring before my reader's eye that noble pile of building. Within, I doubt not, are
rooms of state, old tapestry, painting and sculpture. and por-
traits of the dead, connected with many a tale of deep interest:
—but I cannot linger here.—Look from the windows! far

across the widely-spreading channel to the distant mountains, and nearer, are hill and dale, and wood, and that rapid sparkling stream, turning many a mill, and rushing on, under its pretty bridge, to the wide sea. Truly it was a fair domain, that William bestowed, seven centuries ago, on his brave Baron Mohun. The Norman castle he erected here, with its simple round tower, and long lines of heavy masonry, how different from the present tasteful pile! And the Baron! would I could see him with my mind's eye, with his long spear, and his coat of mail. And yet I am so much of a woman, that I take still more interest in his fair Maude.—A noble and a tender spirit was hers; for when her husband obtained from his prince as the meed of his valour, this broad domain; what think you his lady asked? as many hides of land for the poor, as she could walk round barefooted, in a day. She who could make such a request, would rise with the dawn; and her heroic spirit would carry her on, though wearied and foot-sore, till the late curfew bell :—and as she rested at length in her chamber strewed with rushes, and her maids gathered round and bathed her bleeding feet, her lord would look on her with loving pride, and the poor would rend the air with acclamations. Is it all fancy? perhaps it may be; yet we love to dwell on such a tale, and to indulge the hope, that amid the darkness of the age, she was accepted according to the light she had.

Strange and manifold are the changes that centuries bring; and we found in Sally's humble cottage, comforts and luxuries which the Baron's castle boasted not in the days of Maude; neither would she have found her task so hard a one, could she in her charitable pilgrimage, have travelled a

road as smooth, as level, and as bowery, as the one we now
gaily passed over with Sally, in what she chose to dignify
with the name of a "convenience" but which in fact was neither
more nor less than a covered cart. Sally's cottage *then*, was
not what it is *now*. George has a very good landlord, and
as *he* would tell us, perhaps, he is a very good tenant too ;—
certainly I think he and Sally well deserving of all the kind
consideration their landlord has bestowed. The substantial
porch, the Gothic windows with their stone mullions, the ornamented chimney ; the tasteful garden fence, make almost a
"cottage orné" of Sally's dwelling. I thought it so pretty,
that I have given it you in the frontispiece, as it was
then, and as it still remains. *Then* it was a mere cottage,
but so nice, in such perfect order, so full of all home comforts, that as our dear nurse kissed us, and bid us welcome, we felt that "godliness is profitable for the life that
now is, as well as for that which is to come," and that "the
blessing of God was upon her basket, and her store, upon her
going out, and upon her coming in."

We resolved to make the very most of our three-days-visit,
by seeing all the beauties within our reach ; and by the help
of a stout donkey, we contrived to compass many miles. The
cottage bed, and the early cottage breakfast, were new and
pleasant to us. We were young, and not fastidious, and with
light hearts and ready hands, we proceeded to help Sally in
her arrangements. I think it was a goose she had provided
for the first day's dinner, and two puddings, I know there
were :—a fruit pudding entrusted to our management, and a
plum-pudding which Sally *would* make *herself*, because she
"didn't think we should put in *figs* enough !" Then, when

all these important matters were put in train, and Sally had
given her various instructions to the friendly neighbour, who
was to look to the house, and roast the goose, away we went.
There was much to be seen and admired near at hand :—the
rustic bridge, the fairy waterfall, and Bossington Mill, which
Sally told us had been "drawn out upon paper many a time."
But it was when we left the immediate neighbourhood of the
village, and, wandering for miles through the quiet country,
without meeting a single human being, mounted the breezy
hills, and gazed round on the rich woods, the peaceful and
shady glades, the mountains rising one beyond the other, till
they terminated in Dunkery Beacon, towering sixteen hundred feet above the sea; it was then we felt into how fair a
portion of His wide Universe, the hand of God had led us;
and beholding all that He had made, acknowledged it with
admiring gratitude to be " very good." I pause in the vain
attempt to give any, the faintest idea of such scenes, yet sit
one moment with me on this jutting grey rock, and I have
done. We have reached it by paths cut along the sides of
the towering hills—paths carpetted with soft green moss, and
bordered with yellow furze and broom ; and now look down,
far, far, through the light aspen trees, to the little boat that
looks no larger than a child's toy upon the beach ; that beautiful beach, varied with promontory and bay, fringed with
wood, and stretching away its fantastic rocks and smooth firm
sands as far as the eye can reach.

I almost wonder, that in the neighbourhood of scenery so
imposing, the seat occupied by Sally's landlord, the good Sir
T——, in whose praises she is so warm, should have been built
on so low a site. But come, there is much worth seeing, and

it is close at hand, only over the road, and through the Lodge : and Sally is on her own ground here, quite proud to show the lions, and to tell us all she knows, and it is much, of the liberal and ready kindness which has founded the schools, and built the almshouses, and shews itself throughout the whole village, in the comfortable dwellings of the tenantry.

It is an elegant abode, though low, and with a thatched roof. The windows opening on the lawn, the shadowing verandah covered with rare creeping plants, give it a character of quiet beauty. Sally valued her great neighbours *then*, but she valued them still more afterwards ; when in the time of her deep affliction, they came with those soothing and kind attentions, so valuable to an invalid, telling of the " balm in Gilead, and of the Physician there ;" leading her thoughts away from the dark grave of her only son, to the sure and certain hope of the heavenly inheritance prepared for him above, through his Redeemer's merits.

Let me look once round Sally's cottage, for I saw it no more. It is a pretty room : the wide window fringed with roses, and looking out upon her spicy border of carnations and lupines ; the clock, the bright warming pan, the waiters, large and small ; and the dresser with all its variety of cups and jugs ; and round the walls in every vacant space, drawings of birds and flowers, sent her by her dear young ladies ; and here on this side table, her large Bible ; and behind the door, her shelf of books, (for Sally is a great reader). Yes, it is pretty ! it is *English.* We were sorry to go ; it was the last visit we made in the neighbourhood. Sally accompanied us some way on our journey homewards ; and, amid our

tears, (for women weep when they part, and they will to the
end of the chapter, though the firmer sex laugh at them for
their pains,) amid our tears, we said " Mind, Sally, you must
come to the wedding."

Yes, dear children, I have done more than my title binds
me to; I have gone on beyond the recollections of my *childhood*;
and one of Sally's young ladies is really going to be married;
and the very first thing she did in preparation for so important an event was to work Sally a cap. I must tell you, I
suppose, a little about the wedding, for I know it is a favourite
subject with young people. It was rather early in the year,
so that our pretty garden did not look quite so gay as we
could have wished; and snowdrops and crocuses, the lilac
heath, which flowers in February, and a few blossoms of the
beautiful camellia, were all the flowers we could procure to do
honor to the bride. It is a somewhat large party that ga-
thers round the altar. The bridegroom looks rather grave,
but perhaps he may have his reasons, (and I always have
maintained in spite of him, that it was a very pretty wedding.)
There were the sisters, and a dear cousin besides; one, two,
three, four, five, six; all dressed alike, and all in white.
Then there was our bachelor friend, ready with a kind word
for all, and looking, as he always did, very aristocratic.—The
portly old gentleman from the farm, but not in the new pep-
per and salt suit with silver buttons, which he always declared
he would wear at the wedding, for alas! he is a widower. A
little in the back-ground, are one or two humbler friends,
with Sally at their head, in her pretty new gown, her handsome shawl, and her white satin rosette, looking exactly in
character, *where* she should be, and *as* she should be. And

here in the centre of the group, is an elderly lady, looking on
with much interest, the most richly attired by far, of the
whole party, in an open gown of fawn coloured satin, her
white bonnet and blond fall, all in the most approved style,—
for she has a great idea of having every thing on these occasions, " selon les regles." She is to be mother-in-law to the
bride, (and a very kind and indulgent one she proved
herself.)

Yes, it was a very pretty wedding,—so we all said, when
we talked it over. A few days found the bride in her own
home, a pleasant home, within the compass of a walk, and
Sally was the first who saw her there. She found something
or other, a stray bunch of keys I think it was, which she
thought her poor young lady "must be wanting," and she walked
quietly off to take them to her. Tears do not always tell of
grief.—There was a gush of tears perhaps, when the young
bride heard that Sally was come, and flew down stairs to
welcome her ; but Sally understood it all, and notwithstanding those " nat'ral tears," pronounced in answer to the many
kind enquiries made on her return, that " She was very well,
and she thought, poor thing, she would make herself very
comfortable after a bit." And I believe she did. Sally told
also with pleasure and pride, of the handsome parlour,
with its folding doors ; the Brussels carpet, the curtains of
scarlet moreen, and the many comforts in the new home of
one she loved so well.

Have you ever made one of a wedding-party, and experienced the desolate feeling that creeps over the mind, when
the bride and bridegroom are gone,—the wandering from

room to room,—the constrained attention to the guests who
remain, while the heart is musing on past scenes; the long
day which seems before you? To such a point I am come in
my narrative. Such events as I have yet to tell, are scattered and of little interest; and I feel it will be an act of
courtesy in my reader, if he go on with me to the end.

Years passed on, and another wedding, and another,
followed; till as Sally made her periodical visits to us, she
took the little ones of another generation on her knees, and
in her loving arms. I remember on one occasion it so happened, that the first person she saw on her arrival was one of
these children; a little one between two and three years old.
Sally was muffled up in substantial shawls and cloaks, and
burthened with her basket and bundle; and the child stood
and stared at her, as something unusual : " You don't know
me, my dear," she said, "but I am Sally."—It was enough—
young as the little creature was, she had heard of Sally.—
She turned about, and away she stumped, up the long stair-
case, putting, as children do, one foot ever foremost, and
came panting and laughing to tell us, that Sally was come.
Poor little thing! she might have been run over in the rush
that followed, had not a kind and strong arm lifted her up,
and ran rejoicing with her down the stairs she had mounted
so patiently.

Sally's life was not free from care,—far from it; but I
have dwelt mostly on our *holidays*,—our seasons of happy
intercourse,—the *pleasures* we enjoyed together. " Ah, my
dear, " she said, with a moistened eye, as some notice was
taken of her neat slate coloured gown; "I haven't been to say

out of mourning for these seven years now; first one, and
then another." So it must be if we live on. As I have read
somewhere, "The loss of friends is the tax we pay for lon-
gevity." Sally had trials too in her family. She had a sister
who lived in our neighbourhood, suffering under troubles
which all Sally's kind sympathy and help could do but little
to alleviate. She had been brought up in the same careful
and orderly way,—had been much respected in her place;
and like Sally, had married from it. Her husband was a
sergeant; a gayer bridegroom, I dare say, than Sally's blacksmith; but "Time tries tryst;" and years as they came and
went, brought such trials to poor Fanny, as dimmed *her*
eye, and brought tears of kind sympathy into her sister's.
Other trials Sally had, but her blessed spirit of submission to
the will of God, and her calm and cheerful temper, lightened
them all; and except after her great affliction, the death of her
only son, I do not remember seeing her very much distressed at
any time. Many are the simple pleasures we have enjoyed in
company with her. Once in every visit we had what we called
Sally's feast. A most simple affair it was, a little fruit; a rich
cake of her purchasing; a bottle of ginger or gooseberry wine.
—This was all, but so it was, that from occurring time after time,
and bringing round one table the same dear familiar faces, it
came to be a thing looked forward to, and delighted in. And
pleasant it was, Oh very pleasant! so to assemble in a warm
summer-evening, in our quiet bower. A pretty place is our
bower, with its gothic windows, and door-way of knotted
wood; its shells and alabaster stones, and at its entrance our
bright scarlet geraniums, and the pure arum lifting high its
snowy blossom. Oh very pretty! and spacious too, or so
many could not have sat round the table at Sally's feast.

There was *one* amongst us, whom circumstances had taken to
a distant home, and she had mingled in other scenes; but
her heart beat true to the dear claims of her early home.
Will you read some lines she wrote, and entitled them

## SALLY'S FEAST?

With the titled and great I have sat at the board,
When the feast was spread and the wine cup was poured;
And have heard the soft notes of the light guitar,
In the halls where the fair and the noble are.

I looked around, and there was but one,
That my eye might fondly rest upon ;
And ever I loved at his side to be,
But Oh! it was not the scene for me.

I looked ; and a busy thought would come,
Of the far away, and my childhood's home ;
And a feast ;—Oh fitter by far for me,
That we spread in the garden under the tree.

Under the tree, or away in the bower,
On some sweet soft evening at twilight hour ;
To " Sally's Feast," as in days gone by,
We all came trooping merrily.

It has ever been spread in our joyous hours,
When the days were longest and brightest the flowers ;
And some absent one had been fondly prest,
Once, once again to a parent's breast!

And Sally had come from afar to see,
The group that had circled round her knee;
And free was her heart, and open her hand,
And we loved to come to the feast she had planned.

And we loved to hear of the days gone by,
But shrined in her heart so faithfully ;
When our father was young and our mother a bride,
And their first, first darling was Sally's pride.

Oh Sally's Feast ! it is better than all
The pomp and the pageant of courtly hall.
Away in the bower, or under the tree,
Oh that is the feast that is fitting for me.

But the last, last time thy loving eye,
Shone through the tear-drop mournfully ;
And we knew that thy thoughts away were gone,
To the far off grave of thy only one.

And the last, last time, Oh ! methought it is o'er,
And they who meet now, shall meet here no more ;
Oh scarce it may be, from the west and the east,
We should meet thus again at Sally's feast.

We are journeying on :—it is well ! it is well ;
Thus often of partings and death to tell;
Oh I never can think of the dear ones I love,
But I long to be with them in Heaven above.

Now my kind reader, I pray you pardon me this long
page of verse. Will you go with me before we part, once

more to our dear old village ? Our kind friends there had not
forgotten us, nor we them, and we had met at intervals, but one
visit, paid many years after our residence there, seems fresher
in my mind than any other.  We were a large party, and
there was one sweet little creature with us, we called her the
baby, but she could walk, and talk, and laugh ;—a merry
darling, with firm smooth rosy cheeks, and dark bright eyes,
and brown hair combed straight on her fair forehead, and
chubby arms that she clasped tight round your neck, when
she gave you one of her "good kisses."—Oh how I love such
little dear ones !—

> "Gay, guileless, sportive, lovely little things,
> "Playing around the den of sorrow, clad
> "In smiles ; believing in their fairy hopes,
> "And thinking man and woman true.—all joy,
> "Happy all day, and happy all the night."

Lift up the little one to the window of the carriage, and as
we drive thus early through the wide city, shew her the gay
signs, "the Castle" and "the Beehive"—rosy Bacchus on
his cask, and Brobdignag pattens and hats.  It is a curious
scene, such preparations for the busy day, as tell that this is
indeed a work-day world :  such dusting and cleaning, such
festooning with gay ribbon in the milliners' windows ;  and
see how the waggon loads of fruit and vegetables pour in from
the country!  and how busy the old women are with their tea-
equipages at the corners of the streets, pouring out smoking
potations for the chance customer.  Yes, it is a curious busy
scene, but we have passed it all, and are in the quiet country,
—not quite country either, for here on this "Coronation

Road," is a scene which the mere country could never present. The stately city we have left, with its many towers and steeples, the shipping, a forest of masts reaching up into the very heart of the city; its grave cathedral, and its princely mansions, all seen through a light screen of beautiful foliage. In the foreground, the gaol, a building so handsome and appropriate as almost to reconcile you to its presence, and a row of pretty houses, full of scent and blossom : then away to the left, high above the city, are stately crescents and parades, gleaming in the morning sun; the river, the rocks, and the deep back-ground of wood. A turn in the road, and all is vanished, and we are fairly in the road to Y——. We have travelled over it before, and from village to village all remains much as it was. The bowery lanes, how well I know them all, with here and there a walnut-tree throwing the flickering shadow of its broad leaves on a patch of old grey wall, gay with moss and lichen, and crowned with a wreath of the beautiful crane's-bill, with its bright crimson leaves. It was the first Tuesday in May, the day of the club; but, with childhood, had passed away our admiration of blue wands, and cockades with silver fringe, so we left our visit to Y—— till the afternoon, and staid to dine with old Sarah. Poor Sarah! she gladly welcomed us to her daughter Lyddy's cottage, and put together a round table and a square one; and arranged the cold provisions we had brought with us. Lyddy is but sickly, and looks anxiously upon her four little children. This can never be *her* bonnet with such smart ribbons, hanging against the wall.—Oh no! it is her younger sister Lizzy's, and she is going with her mother to the fair in the afternoon. It is almost too smart, but I believe I must forgive her, especially as she has on a thundering pair of new

seal-skin shoes, which I will venture to say are paid for. A
visit or two more, Lizzy! to Y—— fair, in a new cotton
gown and smart straw bonnet, and then perhaps, like poor
Lyddy, a scantier wardrobe and a paler face, and little ones
to care for. All is well in its season, so you pray in all to be
kept out of temptation. And now away to Y——. There is
the turning that leads up to Cadbury. I wonder if old William
lives yet in that lane. He was a stone-cutter, and how we
used to delight in standing at his open window, or rather
door, to watch the progress of his work—his " grave" work of
carving tomb-stones. The old man would look up over his
spectacles, give a nod of recognition to the well known group,
and proceed with his work, and beautiful we thought it, especially when he came to lay the brickdust on the cherubim's
cheeks, and the leaf gold on their wings. Old William was
quite a patriarch. He was the father of nineteen children,
and earnestly desired *one more*, because, as he said, it could
not make much difference any how, and he should like to say
he had had a score. Now come! all down the village street; it
is not very much altered: it is really quite refreshing to see a
place, where, if *intellect* has marched at all, it has been with
so moderate a stride. We are going to drink tea at the very
house where we took refuge when Joe Thomas's cottage was
on fire. Here are many and manifest improvements, but I
almost quarrel with them; I so loved the old place as it was.
I do believe the "settle" is gone, and the old oak table,—
nevertheless, I cannot but be well pleased with the old friends
that gather round us, and the kind welcome they give. Now
for our old house and garden; and here are changes indeed.
In vain we look behind the house for the yard, where stood
the old branching tree, supporting pails and sieves so beauti-

fully white, where stood the puncheon for rain water, in which for three days we children kept an ill fated gold fish, the last of his race, found in the pond which once contained so many. All is gone, and on the spot is built a spacious room, from the low windows of which you pass down the slope into the garden. What a sweet home-view. This pretty rustic bridge, connecting the two pieces of water, the root-house, the flowers, and the lawn. I see no boundary, and though the garden is in reality but small, it seems from hence to extend far away towards the meadows. There are times perhaps, when the delusion is less complete, when the merry hay-makers are abroad in the fields, or the cattle return to their pastures, — but now you may fancy it all one large pleasure ground, stretching away from one green enclosure to another, even to those distant willows. I took thankfully the bouquet of rare flowers offered me from our old garden—but I asked for *one* more, a spray of the little cinnamon roses that grew there so long ago. Now stop at Sarah's cottage on our way home, for the nosegay she promised us of southern-wood, double stocks, and pinks. The evening closes in, and pleasant but sober are our thoughts, as each mile takes us farther from the abode of our merry childhood.

But I began with Sally, and I must end with her. I do not know that her last visit to us was much distinguished from others she had paid us, and yet I love to dwell on its circumstances. Sally is getting old, but she is not infirm: her breath is a little short, and her eyes are dim; but there are many pleasures we can enjoy together yet. We loved to have her with us, and to shew her such things as she could see at no other time. I went with her once to the Zoological Gar-

dens. We met many a gay party, but I drew her arm within
mine, and was proud and pleased to walk round in such company. Look at the monkeys, Sally! oh the frisky merry
creatures! how they crack their nuts, and pelt each other
with the shells; and swing themselves round into most un-
accountable attitudes. Now come and look at the bears—
poor creatures! their retreats in the old cypress trees of North
America were, I doubt not, more to their taste than this wall
of mason-work. Ah! throw them the piece of bun, for they
will not climb for it to-day—they are sulky; and away to
the macaws—the glorious creatures! how proudly they swing
their crested heads to and fro, and spread out their many-
coloured wings and scream with delight or rage, it is hard to
say which. Yet I love better these quiet and elegant creatures, " Demoiselle birds," as they have aptly been called;
look at their long necks and elegant tufted heads; and their
suit of silver grey. Never courtly lady from under the hand
of the most experienced " modiste," looked half so elegant.
Mind the elephant! he is going to sneeze over your new silk
bonnet, and an elephant's sneeze is a sort of shower bath.
And look to your umbrella; elephants do not much study
the wholesomes; I knew one once, that took a fancy to a
brown silk one, and actually swallowed a great part of it.

I shall be off, for I do not much like the neighbourhood,
and besides, though Sally and I went all round, and were not
tired, my reader may be. Sally enjoyed it much, but I know
not if she were not better pleased with the Asylum for the
blind. Hark, they are singing! and how busily they ply
their tasks, and with what a quiet smile do they greet the
voice of praise, and the tone of kind compassion. " Put me

your very best work, Jenny," said the pleasant Matron, " for
I have promised this pen-tray to the kind lady that spoke to
ye the other morning." And Jenny nodded her head, and
worked away with redoubled energy. " Did your new clothes
fit ye my man ?" she said to a fresh healthy looking boy we
met in the large play-ground. " Yes, mistress," he said, " so
soft and warm." But these will do to play in, she rejoined,
come, run about till two o'clock," and away he went, and we
heard his merry laugh as he joined his companions. The
blind, I believe, are generally very cheerful. I have certainly
known several who have been remarkably so— more than
one among *the poor*, full of trust and thankfulness. " You
will be afraid to go," I said to such an one, speaking of a
treat to some school-children, a tea-drinking in a garden, to
which some old women were to be admitted. " Oh dear,
no," she said," if you'd please to give me a ticket, I shall be
as happy as any child there, I am never afraid nor lonesome
*any where*, I hope it is not making too bold to say, that God
will take care of me." The same old woman (a great favo-
rite of mine she is) came one day, and said she thought it her
duty to tell me she was going for a holiday—she had a new
pair of shoes, and some bread and cheese in a little parcel,
and ten shillings; and the man that drove the waggon promised to look to her, and she was going to London, and
thought she should get on very well. And she did get on
very well, and met with kindness from relatives and friends.
The God in whom she trusted, " ordered her goings, that her
footsteps did not slide." The Saviour of blind Bartimœus
was *her* Saviour, and she went out and came in in safety.

It was pleasant to go with Sally to our Sunday School,—

not down the road, but through the home-field, and these shady lanes. We shall be just in time to see the train of orderly girls come with their kind teachers, into the boys school, and sing their psalm. Stand here, Sally, on this raised step; you will see better, and it is a pleasant sight. The innocence of childhood ;—no, that will not do—it is as great a fable as the age of gold.—No, they are like ourselves —guilty, depraved; " every imagination of their hearts is only evil, and that continually." But we tell them of the Saviour *we* have found; we lead them to " the fountain opened for sin and for uncleanness;" and we love to know that here at least, on this holy Sabbath day, their voices are attuned to a hymn of praise. Who stands *there*, so full of energy among the boys? gravely chiding one, encouraging another, singing with melody in his heart unto the Lord; a great favourite he seems with that nice class of elder boys, and I do not wonder, for he is much their friend, both in temporal and spiritual things. May a blessing rest abundantly on such labourers in the vineyard. Where will he be to-morrow? I dwell on my subject, for he sets us a bright example. He will be up betimes, and in Wordsworth's simple language,—

" He will work cheerily till the day is done."

He will go forth with the health and spirits and talents God has graciously bestowed on him; he will provide for his own household, " things honest in the sight of all men :" and when at length " it ringeth to even song," he will return to his gentle wife, and his laughing loving children, and end his day with the voice of prayer and praise.

Come now, dear Nurse, you shall kneel with us at the table of the Lord, and receive the pledges of His love from

the hands of your old and honoured master ; and kind will be
his greeting to you as we pass into our garden under the old
chestnut-trees. Such were some of our quiet pleasures. Sally's
last visit was not a long one, but we made the most of it. "Will
Sally come up, I wonder," one of us said. " No, not till
you send for her." And it was even so. There is a modest
sense of propriety about her, that some can never learn, and
that seems born with others. In the words that occur in one of
Bean's admirable prayers, she " knows her place, and is
happy and useful in it." But her place was with us then, in
our pleasant school-room. Places and things retain their
names after their use has passed away, and we called it the
school-room still. A busy and varied scene it was, and memory will often go back to those who met there in that pleasant summer-tide. Sisters were there, enjoying the pleasant
and unrestrained intercourse which befits such a relationship.
Scattered books, and drawings, and work, told of industry
and skill. On a couch lay the dear child to whom I inscribe
these pages ; pale and weak, recovering slowly from the long
illness with which it had pleased God to afflict her ; but able
to enjoy the amusing scene. And there was a little mother-
less one, putting stitch after stitch into an everlasting little
bag she was making, or pricking away at a little bird we had
drawn for her with a cherry in its mouth. A loving and
pleasant child, a baby herself, but patronising one still
younger in a most amusing way, calling the little guest "You
tiny little creature, you darling Agnes." She told us she
should stay ill *Septober ;*—a month which I suppose she has
found in the calendar, for the little dear is gone. We had a
merry lad too, among us, in and out at window or door, as
pleased him best ; now for five minutes reading or drawing,

and then away to the garden to bring us a great cabbage-leaf
full of currants and gooseberries. Another too there was,
who had made himself at home in that room many a long
year before ; and Sally (and she is a judge,) pronounced him
to be a " most lively and pleasant gentleman." It was during
this last visit, that our dear father's eye glanced round the
table one day as we were sitting down to dinner. Though
a rather large party, there were none there but his own children and grandchildren; and he said " Where is Sally ?
call her to dine with us." And with the ready courtesy of
the Christian and the gentleman, he went himself to fetch
her, and placed her at his side. It was a sight we loved to
look upon; but there were touching thoughts connected with
it. A tear was in Sally's eye, as she raised the glass to the
health of her honored master ; and her voice faltered as she
looked round, and prayed for a blessing on him and on his
children's children.

And now I fear this must be what I know children
dislike, what they even say " they never can bear,"—a book
without an ending. But what can I do ? I told you my
children, it was a *true* story, and so it is. Sally is living yet,
under the shade of her walnut-trees, and how can I tell you
the end ? I might fancy it. God is often pleased even in this
changing world, to grant a measure of stability to those who
rest satisfied with the place he has appointed for them. He
often provides even here, a quiet dwelling house, and a sure
resting place for his servants; and I think it very probable,
that in his great mercy, no material change may take place in
the circumstances of our dear nurse ; but that respected by
her superiors, and useful among her neighbours, she may live

on to a good old age, in the cottage she has occupied so long; amid scenes familiar to her. It is probable,—but I am content to leave the matter, and so is *she*, to him who has said "And even to your old age, I am He, and even to hoar hairs I will carry you."—And so, dear children, farewell! Some of you wish perhaps, you had some such friend as Sally. But without indulging fruitless wishes, look round on the connections God has given you, with a humble and a thankful heart. Have you duly cherished them? It may be a parent, a sister, a "faithful Nurse," who has the charge of you; and be it which it may, you little know the care and anxiety such a charge involves. If a tended and a cherished one, beware: earthly friends, the best and the dearest, must pass away; wherefore love them truly, obey them implicitly, but pray to be the adopted child of a heavenly Father, and set your best affections upon Him. Have I entertained you? Oh I would gladly do more. I would help you to look beyond this present world, its changes and its chances, to one of unfading glory, where partings can never come; where, as in a secure haven, as in a sheltered fold, you may dwell in peace for ever, accepted, saved, and blessed, through Jesus your Redeemer.

# HOME.

Our Childhood's Home, our Childhood's Home,
  Oh, it seemeth bright and sweet,
When over its daisied turf we bound,
  With small and glancing feet;
And o'er us our Mother spreads her wing,
Like to an angel ministering.

The Home of our Youth is tranquil and blest,
  And we love its quiet hours,
Roving away from sweet to sweet,
  Like bees among the flowers;
In all things around us—within—above,
Reading the depths of a parent's love.

We love it all with a quiet love;
  But oh, 'tis in after times,
That the heart looks back from a selfish world,
  Its passions its cares, and crimes;
And we long with a yearning we knew not before,
For the distant Home that is ours no more.

The social hearth, and the house of God,
   And the calm and earnest prayer,
The shrine of all pure and holy thoughts,
   The dear and the blest are there.
Oh, I marvel not that by night and day,
Thou should'st think of such treasures far away.

Still be it so ;—'mid each changing scene,
   It is well that thy thoughts should roam
From the shadowy darkness the world doth cast,
   To thy Fathers' blessed HOME ;
Longing in mirthful joy to bound,
O'er the field, and the hill, and the garden-ground.

But there's a Home in the world above,
   Far better than ought below.
Oh! be it thine, through a Saviour's love,
   The Way and the Truth to know ;
Till thou reach in Glory that blissful shore ;
That HOME whence the children " go out no more."

THE END.

WARD, PRINTER, MERCERY LANE, CANTERBURY.

CPSIA information can be obtained
at www.ICGtesting.com
Printed in the USA
BVOW06s2108290317
479796BV00012B/115/P